Activities
for a
Differentiated
Classroom

2

Developed by

Wendy Conklin, M.A.

SHELL EDUCATION

Consultant

Chandra C. Prough, M.S.Ed.
National Board Certified
Newport-Mesa
Unified School District

Contributing Authors

Marilyn Gamoneda

Publishing Credits

Dona Herweck Rice, *Editor-in-Chief;* Lee Aucoin, *Creative Director;*
Don Tran, *Print Production Manager;* Timothy J. Bradley, *Illustration Manager;*
Chris McIntyre, M.A.Ed., *Editorial Director;* Sara Johnson, M.S.Ed., *Senior Editor;*
Aubrie Nielsen, M.S., *Associate Education Editor;* Robin Erickson, *Interior Layout Designer;*
Juan Chavolla, *Production Artist;* Stephanie Reid, *Photo Editor;*
Corinne Burton, M.S.Ed., *Publisher*

Shell Education

5301 Oceanus Drive
Huntington Beach, CA 92649-1030
http://www.shelleducation.com
ISBN 978-1-4258-0734-4
© 2011 by Shell Educational Publishing, Inc.
Reprinted 2012

Table of Contents

Understanding Differentiation

As I conduct workshops with teachers of all ages and grade levels, I hear a familiar tune: *Differentiating curriculum is worrisome and stressful.* I believe this is due to the fact that teachers do not know how to begin differentiating. Their administrators tell them that they must differentiate, but teachers are overwhelmed with the task of doing it because there is not a clear explanation of what to do. Teachers know the theory. They know they need to do it. They just do not know *how* to do it.

The right way to differentiate depends on the unique students in a classroom. To successfully differentiate, teachers must first know their students. Knowing what academic level students are at helps us understand where to begin. When we have students who do not succeed, we find out why they are not succeeding. Then, we look for the type of support that they need to help them learn specific concepts. We make adjustments when students have trouble comprehending material. We look for new ways to present information, new manipulatives that make sense, and opportunities to provide additional support. As our struggling students grow, we can then scaffold the amount of support that we provide so that students continue to grow instead of leaning too heavily on that support. Differentiation is about meeting the needs of *all* students and providing the right amount of challenge for *all* students.

What Should I Differentiate and Why?

Many teachers have heard the terms *content*, *process*, and *product* when it comes to differentiating curriculum, but few have the time to ponder how these words apply to what they do in their classrooms. Below is a chart that briefly defines how we differentiate and why we differentiate.

Differentiating Curriculum

How	Why
Vary the Content (what is taught)	**Readiness** (students are not at the same academic level)
Vary the Process (how it is taught)	**Learning Styles** (students prefer different ways of learning)
Vary the Product (what students produce)	**Interests** (students have different passions)

Differentiation Strategies in This Book

What Differentiation Strategies Can I Use?

Each book in the *Activities for a Differentiated Classroom* series introduces a selection of differentiation strategies. Each lesson in this book uses one of the six differentiation strategies outlined below. The strategies are used across different curriculum areas and topics to provide you with multiple real-world examples.

Differentiation Strategy	Lessons in This Book
Tiered Assignments	• Persuasive Texts—*Language Arts* • Fractions—*Mathematics* • Forces and Motion—*Science* • Reading Maps—*Social Studies*
Tiered Graphic Organizers	• Vocabulary—*Language Arts* • Shapes—*Mathematics* • Animals—*Science* • Historic Figures—*Social Studies*
Multiple Intelligences	• Research—*Language Arts* • Patterns in Nature—*Mathematics* • Parts of a Plant—*Science* • Economics—*Social Studies*
Menu of Options	• Poetry—*Language Arts* • Money—*Mathematics* • Earth, Moon, and Sun—*Science* • Government—*Social Studies*
Choices Board	• Reader's Response—*Language Arts* • Measurement—*Mathematics* • Properties of Matter—*Science* • Natural Resources—*Social Studies*
Leveled Learning Centers	• Punctuation Rules!—*Language Arts* • Number Sense—*Mathematics* • Water Cycle—*Science* • Landforms—*Social Studies*

Tiered Assignments

One way to ensure that all students in a classroom advance—using the same skills and ideas regardless of readiness levels—is to tier lessons. Often referred to as _scaffolding_, tiered assignments offer multilevel activities based on key skills at differing levels of complexity. One example of this is leveled reading texts. All students can learn about the Civil War by reading texts that are leveled according to the different reading abilities in the classroom. You can also provide comprehension questions that are leveled. Each student comes away with essential grade-appropriate skills in addition to being sufficiently challenged. The entire class works toward one goal (learning about the Civil War), but the path to that goal depends on each student's readiness level.

So, how do you tier lessons?

- **Pick the skill, concept, or strategy that needs to be learned.** For example, a key concept would be using reading skills and strategies to understand and interpret a variety of informational texts.

- **Think of an activity that teaches this skill, concept, or strategy.** For this example, you could have students summarize the information and include a main idea in the summary.

- **Assess students.** You may already have a good idea of your students' readiness levels, but you can further assess them through classroom discussions, quizzes, tests, or journal entries. These assessments can tell you if students are above grade level, on grade level, or below grade level.

- **Take another look at the activity you developed.** How complex is it? Where would it fit on a continuum scale? Is it appropriate for above-grade-level learners, on-grade-level learners, below-grade-level learners, or English language learners?

- **Modify the activity to meet the needs of the other learners in the class.** Try to get help from the specialists in your school for English language learners, special education students, and gifted learners. For this example, summarizing with a main idea would be appropriate for on-grade-level students. Above-grade-level students should include supporting details in their summaries. The below-grade-level students will need a few examples provided for their summaries. English language learners will begin with the same examples given to below-grade-level students so that they understand what is expected of them. Then, they will summarize information verbally to you.

Remember, just because students are above grade level does not mean that they should be given more work. And, just because students are below grade level does not mean that they should be given less work. Tiered lessons are differentiated by varying the _complexity_, not necessarily the _quantity_ of work required for the assignment. Likewise, all tiered activities should be interesting and engaging.

Differentiation Strategies in This Book (cont.)

Tiered Graphic Organizers

One way to improve the learning and performance of diverse students across grade levels in a wide range of content areas is by utilizing graphic organizers in classroom lessons. Graphic organizers are visual representations that help students gather and sort information, see patterns and relationships, clarify concepts, and organize information. Graphic organizers have a way of connecting several pieces of isolated information by taking new information and fitting it into an existing framework. Old information is retrieved in the process, and the new information is attached. By using graphic organizers in the classroom, teachers are helping students make connections and assimilate new information with what they already know.

Understanding how the brain works helps us understand why graphic organizers are valuable tools for learning. Educational brain research says that our brains seek patterns so that information can become meaningful. In her book, Karen Olsen (1995) states, "From brain research we have come to understand that the brain is a pattern-seeking device in search of meaning and that learning is the acquisition of mental programs for using what we understand." Other researchers believe that graphic organizers are one of the most powerful ways to build semantic memories (Sprenger 1999). Eric Jensen (1998) states that semantic memory is "activated by association, similarities, or contrasts." Graphic organizers assist students with such necessary connections.

The brain does this by storing information similar to how a graphic organizer shows information. It screens large amounts of information and looks for patterns that are linked together. The brain is able to extract meaning more easily from a visual format like a graphic organizer than from written words on a page. Graphic organizers not only help students manage information, they also offer information in a way that students can understand at a glance. When these connections happen, the brain transfers the information from short-term memory to long-term memory. This means that teachers who use graphic organizers help their students manage all of the information with which they are presented each day.

Because students are at different readiness levels, it makes sense to differentiate lessons with tiered graphic organizers. Some teachers worry that students will copy from other students who have additional examples on their graphic organizers. They also note that some of their students do not like to be singled out with modified work. This can be resolved by assigning groups different types of graphic organizers within one lesson. An example of this would be to give one group Venn diagrams, another group T-charts, and a third group matrices. The information can still be scaffolded as needed, but more discreetly because the organizers are different.

Multiple Intelligences

The multiple-intelligences model is based on the work of Howard Gardner (1983). He has identified nine intelligences, which include verbal/linguistic, logical/mathematical, visual/spatial, bodily/kinesthetic, musical/rhythmic, interpersonal, intrapersonal, naturalist, and existential. Gardner says that everyone possesses each of these intelligences, but in each of us, some intelligences are more developed than others.

Some research suggests that certain pathways of learning are stronger at certain stages of development. Sue Teele (1994) devised a survey titled the "Teele Inventory for Multiple Intelligences." She gave it to more than 6,000 students. Her research found that verbal/linguistic intelligence is strongest in kindergarten through third grade. It declines dramatically thereafter. The logical/mathematical intelligence is strongest in first through fourth grade. It also declines dramatically thereafter. The visual/spatial and bodily/kinesthetic intelligences were shown to be dominant throughout elementary and middle school. In addition, middle-school children also show a preference for musical/rhythmic and interpersonal intelligences. Teele's findings show that if elementary teachers want to use the best strategies, they must present lessons that incorporate verbal/linguistic, logical/mathematical, visual/spatial, and bodily/kinesthetic activities.

The Nine Multiple Intelligences

The **Verbal/Linguistic** child thinks in words. This child likes to write, read, play word games, and tell interesting stories.

The **Logical/Mathematical** child thinks by reasoning. This child likes finding solutions to problems, solving puzzles, experimenting, and calculating.

The **Visual/Spatial** child thinks in pictures. This child likes to draw and design.

The **Bodily/Kinesthetic** child thinks by using the body. This child likes dancing, moving, jumping, running, and touching.

The **Musical/Rhythmic** child thinks in melodies and rhythms. This child likes listening to music, making music, tapping to the rhythm, and singing.

The **Interpersonal** child thinks by talking about ideas with others. This child likes organizing events, being the leader, mediating between friends, and celebrating.

The **Intrapersonal** child keeps thoughts to him- or herself. This child likes to set goals, meditate, daydream, and be in quiet places.

The **Naturalist** child thinks by classifying. This child likes studying anything in nature, including rocks, animals, plants, and the weather.

The **Existential** child reflects inwardly about the ultimate issues in life while learning and interacting with others. This child likes to express opinions.

Differentiation Strategies in This Book *(cont.)*

Menu of Options

Providing students the opportunity to choose what activity they want to do increases their level of interest in what they are doing or learning. However, many students do not often get the chance to make choices about their work. It can be challenging and time-consuming for teachers to develop a variety of engaging activities. Yet offering options is essential to getting students interested and motivated in learning. When students are involved in something of their own choosing, they are more engaged in the learning process (Bess 1997; Brandt 1998).

Choices in the classroom can be offered in a variety of ways. Students can choose what they will learn (content), how they will learn (process), and how they will show what they have learned (product). A menu of options is a strategy that differentiates product by giving students the opportunity to choose from a list of highly engaging activities.

The menu of options strategy works well for many reasons. First, it operates much like a menu from a restaurant. A person looking at a menu sees all of the choices. Some cost more and some cost less. No one likes going to a restaurant and being told what to eat. People enjoy choosing what they prefer from the menu. In the same way, a menu of options offers students many different projects from which to choose. These projects are assigned various point values. The point values depend on the amount of work or detail involved in the project. Students must earn a set number of points determined by the teacher, but they can choose which activities they want to complete. Any kind of point system can be used. For example, basic projects that do not take much time can be worth 10 points. Projects that take a moderate amount of time and energy can be worth 30 points. Projects that are very time-consuming can be worth 50 points. If the students need to complete 80 points total, they can get to that total number in many different ways. They may choose a 50-point project and a 30-point project. Or, they may choose two 30-point projects and two 10-point projects.

Secondly, a menu of options is effective because the freedom of choice allows students to complete projects that are of interest to them. This increases the chance that the students will produce high-quality products. Students like to feel in control. When given a list from which to choose, students often choose projects that they like or that fit their learning styles. If the teacher provides enough variety, then all students can find projects that they feel passionate about.

As an alternative to creating a menu of options based on point systems, a teacher can create three or four sections on a menu of options and ask students to choose one project from each section. This strategy is helpful when there are a particular set of concepts that the teacher needs to be sure that students have learned.

Choices Board

Everyone loves to make his or her own choices. Getting the chance to choose what we want increases the chances that we are actually interested in what we are doing or learning. Sadly, students do not always get the chance to make choices. Curriculum plans demand that teachers teach a certain way or about a certain topic. Students have to follow along and pretend to be interested. This does not fool most teachers. One key to getting students engaged in learning is to pique their interests by offering choices. It has been noted that when students are engaged in something of interest or choice, they are more engaged in the learning process (Bess 1997; Brandt 1998). Choices can be given in a variety of ways in a classroom. Choices can be given in what students will learn (content), how they will learn (process), and how they will show what they have learned (product).

Equally important is giving students academically appropriate assignments. Tiering or leveling assignments will ensure that students work on parallel tasks designed to have varied levels of depth, complexity, and abstractness along with varied degrees of scaffolding, support, and direction, depending on each student and the topic. All students work toward one goal, concept, or outcome, but the lesson is tiered to allow for different levels of readiness and performance. As students work, they build on their prior knowledge and understanding. Tiered assignments are productive because all students work on similar tasks that provide individual challenges. Students are motivated to be successful according to their own readiness levels as well as their own learning preferences.

Choices boards combine both choices and tiering by giving students the opportunities to choose leveled activities from a larger list. The difficulty levels of the activities vary.

△ above-grade-level students (shown by a triangle)

☐ on-grade-level students (shown by a square)

◯ below-grade-level students (shown by a circle)

☆ English language learners (shown by a star)

There should be at least two of each leveled activity so that students have an option. A teacher controls the levels of the activities, while students control which activity they will complete within that level. For example, when giving an on-grade-level student an assignment, the teacher may tell the student to choose any square activity from the choices board, and then challenge himself or herself by choosing a triangle activity.

Differentiation Strategies in This Book (cont.)

Leveled Learning Centers

Providing academically appropriate assignments for students is important. All students need to be sufficiently challenged so that they can continue to increase their knowledge. If assignments are too easy, students will be bored and they will not learn anything new. If assignments are too difficult, students will experience stress, which can also deter the learning process.

Leveling, or tiering, assignments will ensure that all students work on parallel tasks designed to have varied levels of depth, complexity, and abstractness along with differing degrees of scaffolding, support, and direction depending on each student and the topic. All students work toward one goal, concept, or outcome, but the lesson is tiered to allow for different levels of readiness and performance. As students work, they build on their prior knowledge and understanding. Tiered assignments are productive because all students work on similar tasks that provide individual challenges. Students are motivated to be successful according to their own readiness levels as well as their own learning preferences.

When possible, teachers should also look for ways to offer students choices. When students are given a chance to choose their activities, they are likely to be more engaged in the learning process (Bess 1997; Brandt 1998).

Leveled learning centers combine the best of both worlds—choices and tiered assignments. Leveled learning centers are centers with activities that are leveled according to academic difficulty. Each student is given a choice to work at any of the centers. The following are some best practices for using leveled learning centers:

- There should be at least three centers to choose from.

- Within each center, there are activities that are appropriate for below-grade-level students, on-grade-level students, and above-grade-level students.

- The varying activity levels can be indicated by different shapes:

    △ above-grade-level activities can be identified with a triangle

    ☐ on-grade-level activities can be identified with a square

    ◯ below-grade-level activities can be identified with a circle

    ☆ activities for English language learners can be identified with a star. These activities should contain vocabulary and language support. Partner English language learners with students who are proficient in English for additional support.

Using leveled learning centers also provides busy teachers with unique opportunities for assessment. As students work in their centers, teachers can observe students and document their progress using checklists. Teachers will be able to identify students who need more challenging activities or scaffolded work, and assignments can be quickly adjusted.

Grouping Students

What Grouping Strategies Can I Use?

There are many variables that a teacher must consider when grouping students to create a successful learning environment. These variables include gender, chemistry between students, social maturity, academic readiness, and special needs. Some students will work well together while others will have great difficulty.

In this book, for ease of understanding, readiness levels are represented with a shape (triangle for above-grade level, square for on-grade level, and circle for below-grade level). In a classroom, however, a teacher might want to change the names for leveled groups from time to time. A teacher might use colors, animal names, or athletic team names to group students. For example, a teacher could cut out and distribute three different colors of construction paper squares, with each color representing a different readiness level. The teacher would tell all the "yellow square" students to find partners who also have a yellow square. This way, the teacher creates homogeneous groups while also allowing students to choose partners.

The following grouping strategies demonstrate various ways to group students in a differentiated classroom. This section is included so that you can learn to quickly group your students and easily apply the strategies.

Flexible Grouping

Flexible grouping means that members of a group change frequently. Routinely using the same grouping technique can lead to negative feelings, feelings of shame or a stigma associated with some group levels, lack of appropriate instruction, boredom, and behavior problems in the classroom. Flexible grouping can change the classroom environment daily, making it more interesting. It takes away the negative feelings and stigma of the struggling students because groups are always changing. No longer are the struggling students always in the same group.

Flexible grouping can occur within one lesson or over an entire unit. Try to modify groups from day to day, week to week, and unit to unit. Flexible grouping can include partner work, cooperative grouping, and whole-class grouping. Students' academic levels, interests, social chemistry, gender, or special needs can determine their placement in a particular group. Organize charts like the ones on the following pages to help you keep track of how you are grouping your students.

Grouping Students (cont.)

What Grouping Strategies Can I Use? (cont.)

Homogeneous Grouping

Homogeneous grouping brings together students who have the same readiness levels. It makes sense to group students homogeneously for reading groups and for language and mathematics skills lessons. To form groups, assess students to determine their readiness levels in a content area. Then, order students from highest to lowest in readiness, and place them in order on a three-row horizontal grid.

One way to create homogeneous groups is by using the chart below. Notice that students in the same row have similar readiness levels.

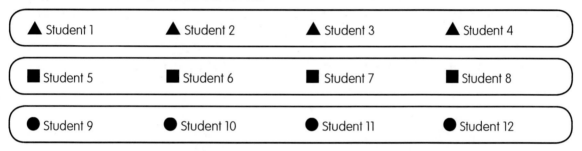

Homogeneous groups share similar readiness levels.

Heterogeneous Grouping

Heterogeneous grouping combines students with varied academic readiness levels. When grouping heterogeneously, look for some diversity in readiness and achievement levels so students can support one another as they learn together.

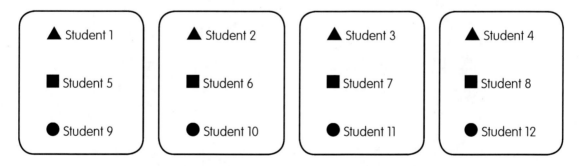

Heterogeneous groups have varying readiness levels.

Another strategy for heterogeneous grouping is to group by interest. Interest groups combine students with varied levels of achievement to create groups that have common interests. Other strategies for heterogeneous grouping include allowing students to self-select their groups, grouping by locality of seating arrangements in the classroom, and selecting groups at random.

Grouping Students (cont.)

What Grouping Strategies Can I Use? (cont.)

Flexogeneous Grouping

Flexogeneous grouping allows for the flexible grouping of homogeneous and heterogeneous groups within the same lesson. Students switch groups at least one time during the lesson to create another group. For example, the homogeneous groups meet for half the lesson and then switch to form heterogeneous groups for the rest of the lesson.

One easy flexogeneous grouping strategy is to jigsaw or mix up already established homogeneous groups. To jigsaw groups, allow homogeneous groups of students to work together for part of the lesson (circle, square, and triangle groups). Then, distinguish group members by labeling them *A*, *B*, and *C* within the same group. All of the *A*s form a new group, the *B*s form a new group, and the *C*s form a new group.

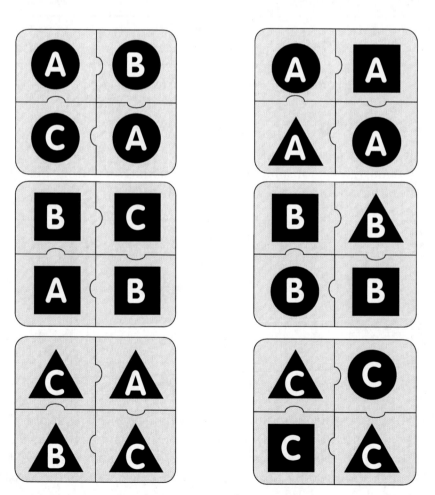

Flexogeneous grouping uses homogeneous and heterogeneous groups in a single lesson.

Working with English Language Learners

Strategies for Working with English Language Learners

Use visual media as an alternative to written responses. Have all students express their thinking through visual media, such as drawings, posters, or slide shows. This is an effective strategy for eliciting responses from English language learners. This also fosters creativity in all students, challenges above-grade-level students, provides opportunities for artistically inclined students who may struggle academically, and avoids singling out English language learners.

Frame questions to make the language accessible. At times, you will need to rephrase questions to clarify meaning for English language learners. Framing questions makes the language accessible to all students. Higher-order questions can be asked without reducing their rigor. Pose questions for English language learners with question stems or frames.

Example Question Stems/Frames

- What would happen if…?
- What is your opinion?
- Why do you think…?
- How would you prove…?
- Would it be better if…?

- How is _____ related to _____?
- If you could _____, what would you do?
- Can you invent _____?
- Why is _____ important?
- Why is _____ better than _____?

Give context to questions to enable understanding. This can be done by placing pictures or small icons directly next to key words. English language learners also benefit from chunking sentences. For example, with the question *In the ocean, how do wind and ocean currents make boats move?* English language learners can see right away that the question is about the ocean, so they have a context for answering the question.

Provide English language learners with sentence stems or frames to encourage higher-order thinking. These learners need language tools to help them express what they think. Sentence stems or frames will not only get the information you need and want from your English language learners, but it will also model how they should be speaking. You can provide these sentence stems or frames on small sticky notes for students to keep at their desks, or write them on laminated cards and distribute them to students, when necessary.

Example Sentence Stems/Frames

- This is important because…
- This is better because…
- This is similar because…
- This is different because…

- I agree with _____ because…
- I disagree with _____ because…
- I think _____ because…
- I think _____ will happen because…

Partner up, and let partners share aloud. Have English language learners work with language-proficient students to answer questions, solve problems, or create projects. Language-proficient partners can provide the academic vocabulary needed to express ideas. Prepare your language-proficient students to work with language learners by explaining that they must speak slowly and clearly and give these learners time to think and speak.

Working with English Language Learners *(cont.)*

How Can I Support English Language Learners?

All teachers should know the language-acquisition level of each of their English language learners. Knowing these levels will help to plan instruction. Using visuals to support oral and written language for students at Level 1 will help make the language more comprehensible. Students at Levels 2 and 3 benefit from pair work in speaking tasks, but they will need additional individual support during writing and reading tasks. Students at Levels 4 and 5 may still struggle with comprehending the academic language used during instruction, as well as with reading and writing. Use the chart below to plan appropriate questions and activities.

Proficiency Levels for English Language Learners—Quick Glance

Proficiency Level	Questions to Ask	Activities/Actions		
Level 1—Entering • minimal comprehension • no verbal production	• Where is…? • What is the main idea? • What examples do you see? • What are the parts of…? • What would happen if…? • What is your opinion?	• listen • point	• draw • circle	• mime
Level 2—Beginning • limited comprehension • short spoken phrases	• Can you list three…? • What facts or ideas show…? • What do the facts mean? • How is _____ related to _____? • Can you invent…? • Would it be better if…?	• move • match	• select • choose	• act/act out
Level 3—Developing • increased comprehension • simple sentences	• How did _____ happen? • Which is your best answer? • What questions would you ask about…? • Why do you think…? • If you could _____ , what would you do? • How would you prove…?	• name • label • tell/say	• list • categorize	• respond (with 1–2 words) • group
Level 4—Expanding • very good comprehension • some errors in speech	• How would you show…? • How would you summarize…? • What would result if…? • What is the relationship between…? • What is an alternative to…? • Why is this important?	• recall • compare/ contrast • describe	• retell • explain • role-play	• define • summarize • restate
Level 5—Bridging • comprehension comparable to native English speakers • speaks using complex sentences	• How would you describe…? • What is meant by…? • How would you use…? • What ideas justify…? • What is an original way to show…? • Why is it better that…?	• analyze • evaluate • create	• defend • justify • express	• complete • support

How to Use This Book

Teacher Lesson Plans

Each lesson is presented in a straightforward, step-by-step format so that teachers can easily implement it right away.

Differentiation Strategies are highlighted for quick reference.

Standards are aligned to grade-level content and English language learner needs.

Materials lists outline items needed for each lesson. If lessons call for slide show software, you might use *Microsoft Powerpoint*® or *Prezi*®. Additional resources are listed on page 167.

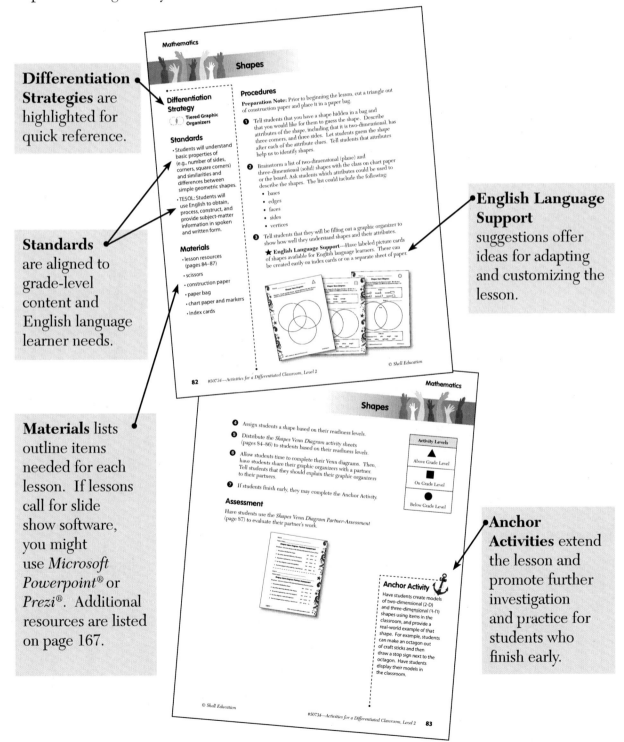

English Language Support suggestions offer ideas for adapting and customizing the lesson.

Anchor Activities extend the lesson and promote further investigation and practice for students who finish early.

How to Use This Book (cont.)

Lesson Resources

These pages include student reproducibles and teacher resources needed to implement each lesson.

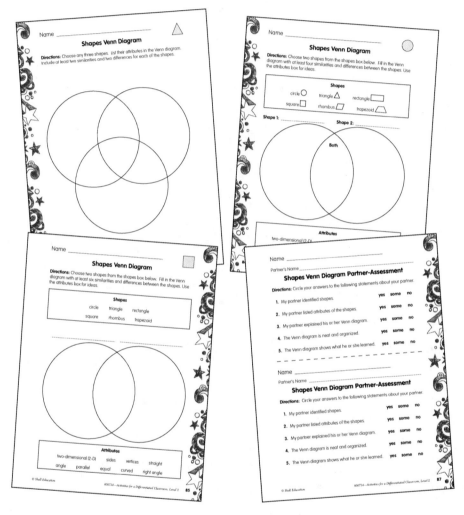

Teacher Resource CD

Helpful reproducibles and images are provided on the accompanying CD. Find a detailed listing of the CD contents on page 168.

- Reproducible PDFs of all student activity sheets and teacher resource pages
- Reproducible PDFs of blank graphic organizers
- Answer key

Correlations to Standards

Shell Education is committed to producing educational materials that are research and standards based. In this effort, we have correlated all of our products to the academic standards of all 50 states, the District of Columbia, and the Department of Defense Dependent Schools.

How to Find Standards Correlations

To print a customized correlation report of this product for your state, visit our website at **http://www.shelleducation.com** and follow the on-screen directions. If you require assistance in printing correlation reports, please contact Customer Service at 1-877-777-3450.

Purpose and Intent of Standards

The No Child Left Behind (NCLB) legislation mandates that all states adopt academic standards that identify the skills students will learn in kindergarten through grade 12. While many states had already adopted academic standards prior to NCLB, the legislation set requirements to ensure the standards were detailed and comprehensive.

Standards are designed to focus instruction and guide adoption of curricula. Standards are statements that describe the criteria necessary for students to meet specific academic goals. They define the knowledge, skills, and content students should acquire at each level. Standards are also used to develop standardized tests to evaluate students' academic progress.

Teachers are required to demonstrate how their lessons meet state standards. State standards are used in the development of all of our products, so educators can be assured that they meet the academic requirements of each state.

McREL Compendium

We use the Mid-continent Research for Education and Learning (McREL) Compendium to create standards correlations. Each year, McREL analyzes state standards and revises the compendium. By following this procedure, McREL is able to produce a general compilation of national standards. Each lesson in this product is based on one or more McREL standards. The chart on page 20 lists each standard taught in this book and the page numbers for the corresponding lessons.

TESOL Standards

The lessons in this book promote English language development for English language learners. The standards listed on page 21, from the Teachers of English to Speakers of Other Languages (TESOL) Association, support the language objectives presented throughout the lessons.

Correlations to Standards *(cont.)*

McREL Standards	Lesson Title	Page
Language Arts		
1.8, Level I: Students will write for different purposes, for example, to entertain, inform, learn, or communicate ideas.	Persuasive Texts	40
3.9, Level I: Students will use punctuation rules in written compositions, for example, using periods after declarative sentences, question marks after interrogative sentences, and commas in a series of words.	Punctuation Rules!	22
4.2, Level I: Students will use a variety of sources to gather information (e.g., informational books, pictures, charts, indexes, videos, television programs, guest speakers, Internet, own observation).	Research	52
5.5, Level I: Students will use a picture dictionary to determine word meaning.	Vocabulary	28
6.1, Level I: Students will use reading skills and strategies to understand a variety of familiar literary passages and texts.	Poetry	46
6.3, Level I: Students will know setting, main characters, main events, sequence, and problems in stories.	Reader's Response	34
Mathematics		
2.3, Level I: Students will understand symbolic, concrete, and pictorial representations of numbers (e.g., written numerals, objects in sets, number lines).	Number Sense	64
2.5, Level I: Students will understand the concept of a unit and its subdivision into equal parts, for example, a whole pizza versus slices of the whole to make fractions.	Fractions	88
4.1, Level I: Students will understand the basic measures of length, width, height, weight, and temperature.	Measurement	76
4.3, Level I: Students will know processes for telling time, counting money, and measuring length, weight, and temperature, using basic standard and nonstandard units.	Money	70
5.1, Level I: Students will understand basic properties of (e.g., number of sides, corners, square corners) and similarities and differences between simple geometric shapes.	Shapes	82
8.2, Level I: Students will extend simple patterns (e.g., of numbers, physical objects, geometric shapes).	Patterns in Nature	58
Science		
1.2, Level I: Students will know that water can be a liquid or a solid and can be made to change from one form to the other while the amount of water stays the same.	Water Cycle	100
3.1, Level I: Students will know basic patterns of the sun and moon.	Earth, Moon, and Sun	94
5.2, Level I: Students will know that plants and animals have features that help them live in different environments.	Parts of a Plant	118
7.2, Level I: Students will know that there are similarities and differences in the appearance and behavior of plants and animals.	Animals	112
8.1, Level I: Students will know that different objects are made up of many different types of materials such as cloth, paper, wood, and metal and have many different observable properties like color, size, shape, and weight.	Properties of Matter	106
10.4, Level I: Students will know that the position and motion of an object can be changed by pushing or pulling.	Forces and Motion	124
Social Studies		
Civics, 2.1, Level I: Students will know that people in positions of authority have limits on their authority (e.g., a crossing guard cannot act as an umpire at a baseball game).	Government	148
Economics, 1.4, Level I: Students will know that people who use goods and services are called consumers, and people who make goods or provide services are called producers, and that most people both produce and consume.	Economics	160
Geography, 1, Level I: Students will understand the characteristics and uses of maps.	Reading Maps	130
Geography, 4.2, Level I: Students will know that places can be defined in terms of their predominant human and physical characteristics.	Landforms	136
Geography, 14.1, Level I: Students will know ways in which people depend on the physical environment.	Natural Resources	142
History, 6.1, Level I: Students will know regional folk heroes, stories, or songs that have contributed to the development of the cultural history of the U.S.	Historic Figures	154

Correlations to Standards (cont.)

	TESOL Standards	Lesson Title	Page
TESOL 1.3	Students will use learning strategies to extend their communicative competence.	Persuasive Texts	40
TESOL 2.2	Students will use English to obtain, process, construct, and provide subject-matter information in spoken and written form to achieve academically in all content areas.	Punctuation Rules!	22
		Vocabulary	28
		Research	52
		Patterns in Nature	58
		Number Sense	64
		Money	70
		Measurement	76
		Shapes	82
		Fractions	88
		Earth, Moon, and Sun	94
		Water Cycle	100
		Properties of Matter	106
		Animals	112
		Parts of a Plant	118
		Force and Motion	124
		Reading Maps	130
		Landforms	136
		Natural Resources	142
		Government	148
		Historic Figures	154
		Economics	160
TESOL 2.3	Students will use appropriate learning strategies to construct and apply academic knowledge.	Reader's Response	34
		Poetry	46

Punctuation Rules!

Differentiation Strategy

 Leveled Learning Centers

Standards

• Students will use punctuation rules in written compositions, for example, using periods after declarative sentences, question marks after interrogative sentences, and commas in a series of words.

• TESOL: Students will use English to obtain, process, construct, and provide subject-matter information in spoken and written form.

Materials

• lesson resources (pages 24–27)

• scissors

• pictures of people from newspapers or magazines

• art supplies

• camera

• printer

Procedures

Preparation Note: Set up three centers in the classroom. Cut apart the *Punctuation Rules!* center activities (page 24) and display the activity sheets in the centers. Place newspaper and magazine pictures at Center 1.

❶ Begin by saying the following sentence using different expressions:

Matter-of-fact statement: "My hair is green today."

Question: "Is my hair green today?"

Exclamation: "My hair is green today!"

❷ Ask students to make up sentences with a partner. Have them practice saying those sentences to each other and have the opposite partner guess what type of sentence they are saying: statement, interrogative, or exclamatory.

❸ Tell students that different types of sentences end with different punctuation marks. Tell students that interrogative sentences end with question marks. For example, "How does the gummy bear taste?" The structure of an interrogative sentence differs from statements and exclamations. Refer students to the interrogative sentence in Step 1. Exclamatory sentences end with exclamation points. For example, "This is delicious!" Declarative sentences end with a period. For example, "My gummy bear is green."

❹ Assign students a shape based on their readiness levels. Each center has activities at three levels.

❺ Explain the directions for each center and let students choose where they would like to work. You can also assign students a center to begin working in and let them rotate as class time permits. Provide students with art supplies to help them complete the activities.

Punctuation Rules!

6 Monitor students' progress as they work and provide assistance as needed.

★ **English Language Support**—Use a camera to take pictures of students using body language to represent statements (hands on hips), questions (tilted head with questioning expression), and exclamations (excited expression with hands in the air). Print out the pictures, label each one on the backside, and use these as flash card reminders for your English language learners.

7 If students finish early, they may complete the Anchor Activity.

Assessment

Observe students as they work at the centers. Use the *Punctuation Assessment Checklist* (page 25) to keep track of student progress.

Activity Levels
▲
Above Grade Level
■
On Grade Level
●
Below Grade Level

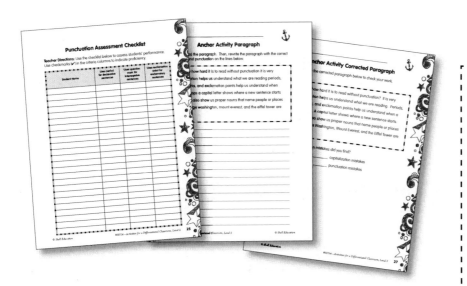

Anchor Activity

Have students read aloud the paragraph on the *Anchor Activity Paragraph* activity sheet (page 26) that has no capitalization or ending punctuation. Then, have students rewrite the paragraph using correct punctuation and capitalization. When they are finished, give students copies of the *Anchor Activity Corrected Paragraph* activity sheet (page 27). Have them check their own version to see if they included all the correct capitalization and punctuation.

Center 1: Statements

△ Choose a picture and write a speech bubble that includes three sentences ending with periods.

▢ Choose a picture and write a speech bubble that includes two sentences ending with periods.

◯ Choose a picture and write a speech bubble that includes at least one sentence ending with a period.

- -

Center 2: Questions

△ Draw a picture of yourself. Write at least four questions that can be answered using your picture.

◯ Draw a picture of yourself. Write one question that can be answered using your picture.

▢ Draw a picture of yourself. Write three questions that can be answered using your picture.

- -

Center 3: Exclamations

◯ Think of a person, place, thing, hobby, sport, or a favorite food that you love. Then, write one sentence about it using an exclamation point.

▢ Think of a person, place, thing, hobby, sport, or a favorite food that you love. Then, write two sentences about it using exclamation points.

△ Think of a person, place, thing, hobby, sport, or a favorite food that you love. Then, write at least three sentences about it using exclamation points.

Punctuation Assessment Checklist

Teacher Directions: Use the checklist below to assess students' performance. Use checkmarks (✔) in the criteria columns to indicate proficiency.

Student Name	Uses period for declarative sentences	Uses question mark for interrogative sentences	Uses exclamation point for exclamatory sentences

Name _____

Anchor Activity Paragraph

Directions: Read the paragraph. Then, rewrite the paragraph with the correct capitalization and punctuation on the lines below.

do you know how hard it is to read without punctuation it is very hard punctuation helps us understand what we are reading periods, question marks, and exclamation points help us understand when a sentence stops a capital letter shows where a new sentence starts capital letters also show us proper nouns that name people or places or things george washington, mount everest, and the eiffel tower are proper nouns

_____

_____

_____

_____

_____

_____

_____

_____

_____

_____

_____

_____

Name _____

Anchor Activity Corrected Paragraph

Directions: Use the corrected paragraph below to check your work.

Do you know how hard it is to read without punctuation? It is very hard! Punctuation helps us understand what we are reading. Periods, question marks, and exclamation points help us understand when a sentence stops. A capital letter shows where a new sentence starts. Capital letters also show us proper nouns that name people or places or things. George Washington, Mount Everest, and the Eiffel Tower are proper nouns.

How many punctuation mistakes did you find?

_____ capitalization mistakes

_____ punctuation mistakes

Vocabulary

Differentiation Objective

 Tiered Graphic Organizers

Standards

- Students will use a picture dictionary to determine word meaning.

- TESOL: Students will use English to obtain, process, construct, and provide subject-matter information in spoken and written form.

Materials

- lesson resources (pages 30–33)

- picture dictionaries (*See page 167.*)

- vocabulary picture cards

Procedures

1 Tell students that you are thinking of a vocabulary word and are going to give them clues to help them guess what it is. Choose a vocabulary word for students to guess.

2 Provide students with the definition of the word and see if they can guess the vocabulary word. Next, provide examples of the word for students to guess, and then provide synonyms for the word. Finally, draw a picture of the word for students.

3 Have students use the new vocabulary word in a sentence. Write their ideas for using the word in a sentence on the board. Point out that there could be many correct answers for how to use the word in a sentence.

4 Tell students that they will be looking up new vocabulary words and completing a vocabulary map. Assign vocabulary words to students. Distribute copies of the *Vocabulary Map* activity sheets (pages 30–32) to students based on their readiness levels. Review the directions with students and answer any questions that they may have.

5 Give students picture dictionaries and time to complete their vocabulary maps. Monitor students as they work and provide assistance as needed.

★ **English Language Support**—Have simple picture dictionaries and picture vocabulary cards available for English language learners. After students finish, allow them to share their favorite new vocabulary word with the class.

6 If students finish early, they may complete the Anchor Activity.

Assessment

Have the students complete the *Vocabulary Self-Assessment* (page 33) to evaluate their work.

Activity Levels
▲
Above Grade Level
■
On Grade Level
●
Below Grade Level

Anchor Activity

Have students make a vocabulary matching game with vocabulary words and definitions using index cards. Students will need to write each word on one card and its definition on a different card. Then, they will mix them up and put them face down. Students will take turns choosing two cards. If the word matches the definition, the student keeps the card. If the cards do not match, then the student puts the cards back down. The student with the most pairs wins.

Name _____

Vocabulary Map

Directions: Choose two new vocabulary words and use a picture dictionary to complete the vocabulary map.

Word:		
Definition:		
Sentence	**2 Antonyms**	**2 Synonyms**

Word:		
Definition:		
Sentence	**2 Antonyms**	**2 Synonyms**

Name _____

Vocabulary Map

Directions: Choose two new vocabulary words and use a picture dictionary to complete the vocabulary map.

Word:

Definition:

Example	2 Synonyms	Picture

Word:

Definition:

Example	2 Synonyms	Picture

Name _____

Vocabulary Map

Directions: Choose two new vocabulary words and use a picture dictionary to complete the vocabulary map.

Word:

Definition	Example	Picture

Word:

Definition	Example	Picture

Name _____

Vocabulary Self-Assessment

Directions: Circle the words and pictures that describe your work.

I learned new vocabulary words.	☺ yes	😐 some	☹ no
The vocabulary map helped me learn.	☺ yes	😐 some	☹ no
I completed my vocabulary map.	☺ yes	😐 some	☹ no
I will use my new vocabulary words.	☺ yes	😐 some	☹ no

I really liked: _____

Next time I want to: _____

— —

Name _____

Vocabulary Self-Assessment

Directions: Circle the words and pictures that describe your work.

I learned new vocabulary words.	☺ yes	😐 some	☹ no
The vocabulary map helped me learn.	☺ yes	😐 some	☹ no
I completed my vocabulary map.	☺ yes	😐 some	☹ no
I will use my new vocabulary words.	☺ yes	😐 some	☹ no

I really liked: _____

Next time I want to: _____

Reader's Response

Differentiation Strategy

Choices Board

Standards

- Students will know setting, main characters, main events, sequence, and problems in stories.

- TESOL: Students will use appropriate learning strategies to construct and apply academic knowledge.

Materials

- lesson resources (pages 36–39)

- scissors

- children's books at students' reading levels (*See page 167.*)

- sticky notes

- art supplies

- pocket chart (*optional*)

- audio recorder (*optional*)

Procedures

Preparation Note: Copy and cut apart the *Reader's Response Choices Cards* activity sheets (pages 37–39) and place them in a pocket chart or on a bulletin board.

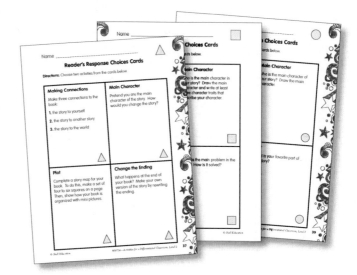

1 Choose a children's book to read aloud to students. As you preview the story title and browse the introductory illustrations, have students think about what may happen in the story. Give each student a sticky note. Tell students to write down a prediction of what will happen in the story on their sticky notes. At the end of the story, have students check their predictions to see if they were correct.

2 As you read the story, tell students to identify the setting, main characters, main events, and problems in the story. When students point out these parts in the story, place a sticky note on that page with the part correctly labeled (e.g., setting, main character).

3 Divide the class into small, homogeneous groups. Assign groups a shape based on their readiness levels.

4 Display picture books at varying reading levels for the class. Tell the students that they will be choosing a story to read and two reader's response activities to complete from a choices board.

Reader's Response

5 Distribute copies of the *Reader's Response Choices Board* activity sheet (page 36) to students so that they can review the activity choices.

6 Direct students to the *Reader's Response Choices Cards* (pages 37–39) that you placed on the pocket chart or bulletin board. Have below-grade-level students choose a circle activity to complete individually and a square activity to complete with a friend in their group. Have on-grade-level students choose a square activity to complete individually and a triangle activity to complete with a friend in their group. Have above-grade-level students choose two triangle activities to complete, one individually and one with a friend in their group. Or, you may distribute copies of the *Reader's Response Choices Cards* to students so that they may choose from activities on their level only. Provide students with art supplies to help them complete the activities.

★ **English Language Support**—Meet with English language learners in small groups to guide them in writing their responses. Or, if possible, allow them to record their answers with an audio recorder.

7 If students finish early, they may complete the Anchor Activity.

Assessment

Make necessary adjustments as students work to be sure they are working at the appropriate level. Assess students' understanding by evaluating their work from the *Reader's Response Choices Board*.

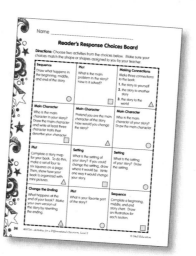

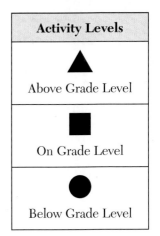

Activity Levels
▲
Above Grade Level
■
On Grade Level
●
Below Grade Level

Anchor Activity

Have students choose a story and rewrite it from the perspective of another character in the book. For example, *Hansel and Gretel* could be written from the perspective of the witch. After writing their stories, students can read them to their classmates.

Name _____

Reader's Response Choices Board

Directions: Choose two activities from the choices below. Make sure your choices match the shape or shapes assigned to you by your teacher.

Sequence Draw what happens in the beginning, middle, and end of the story. ○	**Plot** What is the main problem in the story? How is it solved? ▢	**Making Connections** Make three connections to the book: 1. the story to yourself 2. the story to another story 3. the story to the world △
Main Character Who is the main character in your story? Draw the main character and write at least three character traits that describe your character. ▢	**Main Character** Pretend you are the main character of the story. How would you change the story? △	**Main Character** Who is the main character of your story? Draw the main character. ○
Plot Complete a story map for your book. To do this, make a set of four to six squares on a page. Then, show how your book is organized with mini pictures. △	**Setting** What is the setting of your story? If you could change the setting, draw where it would be. Write one way it would change your story. ▢	**Setting** What is the setting of your story? Draw the setting. ○
Change the Ending What happens at the end of your book? Make your own version of the story by rewriting the ending. △	**Plot** What is your favorite part of the story? ○	**Sequence** Complete a beginning, middle, and end story chart. Draw an illustration for each section. ▢

Name _____

Reader's Response Choices Cards

Directions: Choose two activities from the cards below.

Making Connections

Make three connections to the book:

1. the story to yourself

2. the story to another story

3. the story to the world

Main Character

Pretend you are the main character of the story. How would you change the story?

Plot

Complete a story map for your book. To do this, make a set of four to six squares on a page. Then, show how your book is organized with mini pictures.

Change the Ending

What happens at the end of your book? Make your own version of the story by rewriting the ending.

Name _____

Reader's Response Choices Cards

Directions: Choose two activities from the cards below.

Setting	**Main Character**
What is the setting of your story? If you could change the setting, draw where it would be. Write one way it would change your story.	Who is the main character in your story? Draw the main character and write at least three character traits that describe your character.
Sequence	**Plot**
Complete a beginning, middle, and end story chart. Draw an illustration for each section.	What is the main problem in the story? How is it solved?

Name _____

Reader's Response Choices Cards

Directions: Choose two activities from the cards below.

Setting	Main Character
Setting What is the setting of your story? Draw the setting.	**Main Character** Who is the main character of your story? Draw the main character.
Sequence Draw what happens in the beginning, middle, and end of the story.	**Plot** What is your favorite part of the story?

Persuasive Texts

Differentiation Strategy

 Tiered Assignments

Standards

- Students will write for different purposes, for example, to entertain, inform, learn, or communicate ideas.

- TESOL: Students will use learning strategies to extend their communicative competence.

Materials

- lesson resources (pages 42–45)

- sticky notes

- chart paper and markers

- a children's animal book (*See page 167.*)

- art supplies

- animal picture cards or picture dictionaries

Procedures

❶ Distribute one sticky note to each student. Ask students to vote for their favorite television show by writing its name on the sticky note. Take all the students' votes and stick them on the board. Count the votes to find the top two shows.

❷ On the board, have students list reasons why one of the top two shows is better than the other. Explain to students that they must try to persuade others to vote for one show instead of the other. Use a sheet of chart paper to list all of the reasons on a class T-chart.

❸ Review the students' list of persuasive statements and take another class vote for their favorite television show. Discuss why one show won versus the other (e.g., better persuasive reasons). Explain that this is called a *persuasive argument*, because they are trying to persuade or convince someone to agree with them.

❹ Tell students that they will be listening to a story and writing persuasive reasons why they should get a special pet.

❺ First, read a children's animal book aloud to the class. Then, have students brainstorm reasons why they might want that animal as a pet. Ask students to think about persuasive reasons that they could give their parents to allow them to have that animal as a pet. Record students' responses on a class chart that they can reference as they work on their tiered assignments.

Persuasive Texts

6 Assign students a shape based on their readiness levels. Distribute copies of the *Persuasive Writing* activity sheets (pages 42–44) to students based on their readiness levels. Provide students with art supplies to help them complete the activities.

Activity Levels
▲
Above Grade Level
■
On Grade Level
●
Below Grade Level

★ **English Language Support**—Have animal picture vocabulary cards and picture dictionaries available for English language learners.

7 If students finish early, they may complete the Anchor Activity.

Assessment

Have students complete the *Persuasive Writing Self-Assessment* (page 45) to evaluate their learning.

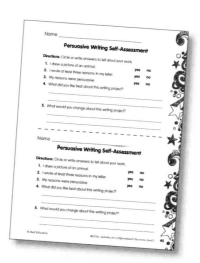

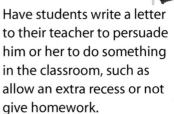

Anchor Activity

Have students write a letter to their teacher to persuade him or her to do something in the classroom, such as allow an extra recess or not give homework.

Name _____

Persuasive Writing

Part 1 Directions: Draw a picture in the box of a pet that you really want.

Part 2 Directions: Think of the reasons why you want the pet, and the reasons why your parent might not want you to have it. Pretend that you are your parent and write a letter to yourself with at least three reasons why you should not get that pet. The reasons should persuade you to change your mind.

Dear _____,

_____

_____

_____

_____

Love,

_____

Name _____

Persuasive Writing

Part 1 Directions: Draw a picture in the box of a pet that you really want.

Part 2 Directions: Write a letter to your parents with at least three reasons why they should give you the pet.

Dear _____,

_____

_____

_____

_____

Love,

_____

Name _____

Persuasive Writing

Part 1 Directions: Draw a picture in the box of a pet that you really want.

Part 2 Directions: Write three reasons why you should get that animal. Explain your reasons to your teacher.

Can I have a/an _____? May I? Please?

Reason 1: _____

Reason 2: _____

Reason 3: _____

Name _____

Persuasive Writing Self-Assessment

Directions: Circle or write answers to tell about your work.

1. I drew a picture of an animal.   **yes**   **no**

2. I wrote at least three reasons in my letter.   **yes**   **no**

3. My reasons were persuasive.   **yes**   **no**

4. What did you like best about this writing project?

   _____

   _____

5. What would you change about this writing project?

   _____

   _____

— —

Name _____

Persuasive Writing Self-Assessment

Directions: Circle or write answers to tell about your work.

1. I drew a picture of an animal.   **yes**   **no**

2. I wrote at least three reasons in my letter.   **yes**   **no**

3. My reasons were persuasive.   **yes**   **no**

4. What did you like best about this writing project?

   _____

   _____

5. What would you change about this writing project?

   _____

   _____

Poetry

Differentiation Strategy

 Menu of Options

Standards

- Students will use reading skills and strategies to understand a variety of familiar literary passages and texts.

- TESOL: Students will use appropriate learning strategies to construct and apply academic knowledge.

Materials

- lesson resources (pages 48–51)

- examples of poetry (couplet, haiku, cinquain, shape poem, acrostic, and sensory poem (*See page 167.*)

- one rhyming poem (*See page 167.*)

- audio recorder or podcast software

Procedures

1 At the end of a unit on poetry, tell students that they will choose different types of poems to write. Review examples of different types of poetry covered in the unit, including couplet, haiku, cinquain, shape, acrostic, and sensory poems.

2 Read a sample rhyming poem to the class. As a class, choose a topic and have students offer words about the topic that rhyme. Model writing a poem by completing a shared writing with the students. Post your class poetry on a poetry bulletin board.

3 Distribute copies of the *Poetry Menu of Options* activity sheets (pages 48–49) to students and explain the projects to them. Model for students how they could select different projects to total 25 points. Set a due date for the projects. Answer any questions that students may have.

★ **English Language Support**—Make modifications for English language learners by allowing them to record their poems instead of writing them. They can use an audio recorder or podcast software to do this.

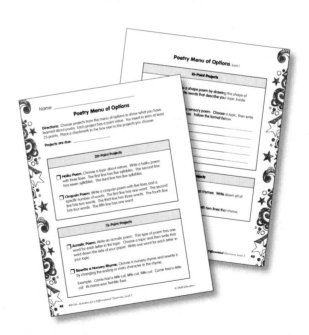

4 Distribute copies of the *Poetry Menu of Options Planning Chart* activity sheet (page 50) to students and allow them time to decide which type of poems that they want to write. Have students fill out their charts.

5 Provide time in class for students to write their poems. When the poems are due, have students present their favorite poem to the class.

6 If students finish early, they may complete the Anchor Activity.

Assessment

Have students complete the *Poetry Self-Assessment* (page 51) to evaluate their learning.

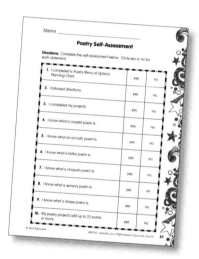

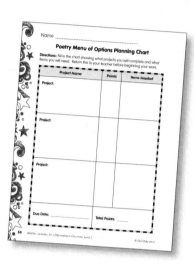

Anchor Activity

Have students write a cinquain poem with five lines of a specific number of syllables, like this:

Line	Syllables
1	2
2	4
3	6
4	8
5	2

Example:

Nanna

Puffy and soft

Humming, baking, loving

Sitting in her lap and reading

Grandma

Name _____

Poetry Menu of Options

Directions: Choose projects from the menu of options to show what you have learned about poetry. Each project has a point value. You need to earn at least 25 points. Place a checkmark in the box next to the projects that you choose.

Projects are due: _____

20-Point Projects

☐ **Haiku Poem:** Choose a topic about nature. Write a haiku poem with three lines. The first line has five syllables. The second line has seven syllables. The third line has five syllables.

☐ **Cinquain Poem:** Write a cinquain poem with five lines and a specific number of words. The first line has one word. The second line has two words. The third line has three words. The fourth line has four words. The fifth line has one word.

15-Point Projects

☐ **Acrostic Poem:** Write an acrostic poem. This type of poem has one word for each letter in the topic. Choose a topic and then write that word down the side of your paper. Write one word for each letter in your topic.

☐ **Rewrite a Nursery Rhyme:** Choose a nursery rhyme and rewrite it by changing the ending or main character in the rhyme.

Example: *Carrie had a little cat, little cat, little cat. Carrie had a little cat. Its name was Twinkle Toes.*

Poetry Menu of Options *(cont.)*

10-Point Projects

☐ **Shape Poem:** Write a shape poem by drawing the shape of your topic. Next, write words that describe your topic inside your drawing.

☐ **Sensory Poem:** Write a sensory poem. Choose a topic, then write one line using each sense. Follow the format below.

I see _____

I hear _____

I taste _____

I smell _____

I feel _____

5-Point Projects

☐ **Rhyming Words List:** Find a poem that rhymes. Write down all of the pairs of rhyming words.

☐ **Couplet Poem:** Write a couplet poem with two lines that rhyme.

Name _____

Poetry Menu of Options Planning Chart

Directions: Fill in the chart showing what projects you will complete and what items you will need. Return this to your teacher before beginning your work.

Project Name	Points	Items Needed
Project:		
Project:		
Project:		

Due Date: _____ **Total Points:** _____

Name _____

Poetry Self-Assessment

Directions: Complete the self-assessment below. Circle yes or no for each statement.

1. I completed a *Poetry Menu of Options Planning Chart.*	yes	no
2. I followed directions.	yes	no
3. I completed my projects.	yes	no
4. I know what a couplet poem is.	yes	no
5. I know what an acrostic poem is.	yes	no
6. I know what a haiku poem is.	yes	no
7. I know what a cinquain poem is.	yes	no
8. I know what a sensory poem is.	yes	no
9. I know what a shape poem is.	yes	no
10. My poetry projects add up to 25 points or more.	yes	no

Research

Differentiation Strategy

Multiple Intelligences

Standards

- Students will use a variety of sources to gather information.

- TESOL: Students will use English to obtain, process, construct, and provide subject-matter information in spoken and written form.

Materials

- lesson resources (pages 54–57)

- chart paper and markers

- children's biographies (*See page 167.*)

- art supplies

Procedures

1 Begin by asking students to name famous people who are living or have lived in the past. As students list these names, ask them to tell you a fact about each person. Record the list of famous people on a sheet of chart paper.

2 Tell students that they will choose a famous person to research. Explain that to find out about these people, they can get information from books, interviews, charts, videos, the Internet, and other places.

3 Show students a sample biography about a famous person. Have students look at the table of contents from that book. Explain to students that the table of contents tells them the main idea of each section. They can find out where to find certain facts about a famous person by looking at the table of contents in a biography. Model this for the class by turning to one of the sections listed in the table of contents and finding a fact about the person.

4 Display the *Research Bibliography* activity sheet (page 54) and tell students that they will use this sheet to list the places that they find their information about a famous person. Explain to students that a list of information sources is called a *bibliography*.

5 Write the title of the biography that you shared with the class in the Source 1 box on this sheet. Show students how to find the author of the book and list it on the bibliography. Next, show students how to find the date of publication and list it on the bibliography. Finally, write the fact that you learned from the book on the space provided in the activity sheet.

6 Explain to students that they will research a famous person. They will find facts about this person from different sources. Two sources will be books and one source will be a website.

Research

7 Distribute copies of the *Research Bibliography* activity sheet (page 54) to students, and remind them that this is where they will record their research findings. Distribute copies of the *Research Project Parent Letter* (page 56) to students to take home. Schedule time to go to the library and the computer lab to allow students to conduct their research. Or, have students conduct their research at home. Set a due date for the project and have students fill in the date on the parent letter.

★ **English Language Support**—Assign a "buddy" to each English language learner when the class visits the library. The teacher and the buddy can assist the learner with identifying at least one (preferably two) source(s) of library material for the research project. As the teacher, offer a five-minute interview to each English language learner so that you can be one source of information on their topic.

8 Tell students that after they have completed their research, they will choose one project to complete and present to the class. Distribute copies of the *Multiple Intelligences Research Projects* activity sheet (page 55) to students, and review the options as a class. Encourage students to choose the project that appeals the most to them. Provide students with art supplies to help them complete the activities.

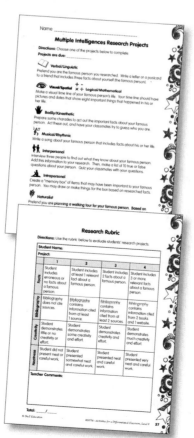

9 After the research projects are due, allow students time to share their projects with the class.

10 If students finish early, they may complete the Anchor Activity.

Assessment

Use the *Research Rubric* (page 57) to evaluate students' projects.

Anchor Activity

Have students research the history of their favorite sport. Students should find out how it started, where it started, when it started, and what famous people started it. Have students draw an item needed for the sport and write their research findings around it.

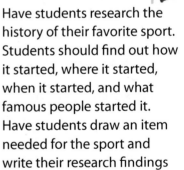

Name _____

Research Bibliography

Directions: Find three facts about a famous person from three different sources. Two sources need to be books and one source needs to be a website. Record the information, in the boxes below, showing where you found these facts.

Source 1 (book)

Title of the book:

Author:

Date of publication:

Fact I learned:

Source 2 (book)

Title of the book:

Author:

Date of publication:

Fact I learned:

Source 3 (website)

Title of the website:

URL:

Date I viewed the website:

Fact I learned:

Name _____

Multiple Intelligences Research Projects

Directions: Choose one of the projects below to complete.

Projects are due: _____

 ### Verbal/Linguistic

Pretend that you are the famous person you researched. Write a letter or a postcard to a friend that includes three facts about yourself (the famous person).

 ### Visual/Spatial   +   -   × ÷   Logical/Mathematical

Make a visual time line of your famous person's life. Your time line should have pictures and dates that show eight important things that happened in his or her life.

 ### Bodily/Kinesthetic

Prepare some charades to act out the important facts about your famous person. Act these out, and have your classmates try to guess who you are.

 ### Musical/Rhythmic

Write a song about your famous person that includes facts about his or her life.

 ### Interpersonal

Interview three people to find out what they know about your famous person. Add this information to your research. Then, make a list of 10 true or false questions about your person. Quiz your classmates with your questions.

 ### Intrapersonal

Create a "memory box" of items that may have been important to your famous person. You may draw or make things for the box based on researched facts.

 ### Naturalist

Pretend you are planning a walking tour for your famous person. Based on facts you learned about his or her life, make a list of the places you would take that person and why you think he or she would enjoy those places.

Research Project Parent Letter

Date _____

Dear Parent(s),

    Your child will be working on a research project about a famous person. Please assist your child in choosing a famous person to research and in completing a project about that person.

    Students will need to find three facts about the famous person. They should use nonfiction books and the Internet to gather information. Students will record where they found their facts on the *Research Bibliography* activity sheet. Then, they will choose a project from the *Multiple Intelligences Research Projects* list to complete and present to the class.

    Students will have time in class to work on their research, but they may need to spend additional time at home on their research. The project will need to be completed at home. This research project is due on

_____.

Sincerely,

_____

Research Rubric

Directions: Use the rubric below to evaluate students' research projects.

Student Name:				
Project:				
	1	**2**	**3**	**4**
Facts	Student includes erroneous or no facts about a famous person.	Student includes at least 1 relevant fact about a famous person.	Student includes 2 facts about a famous person.	Student includes 3 or more relevant facts about a famous person.
Bibliography	Bibliography does not cite sources.	Bibliography contains information cited from at least 1 source.	Bibliography contains information cited from at least 2 sources.	Bibliography contains information cited from 2 books and 1 website.
Creativity	Student demonstrates little or no creativity or effort.	Student demonstrates some creativity and effort.	Student demonstrates creativity and effort.	Student demonstrates much creativity and effort.
Neatness	Student did not present neat or careful work.	Student presented somewhat neat and careful work.	Student presented neat and careful work.	Student presented very neat and careful work.
Teacher Comments:				

Total: _____/_____

Patterns in Nature

Differentiation Strategy

 Multiple Intelligences

Standards

- Students will extend simple patterns.

- TESOL: Students will use English to obtain, process, construct, and provide subject-matter information in spoken and written form.

Materials

- lesson resources (pages 60–63)
- several stuffed animals of one type (e.g., dogs)
- chart paper and markers
- audio recorders
- art supplies
- digital camera
- printer
- posterboard

Procedures

1 Bring in a set of one kind of stuffed animal (for example, dogs) to show to the class. Ask students if they notice any groups of numbers. They may point out that the dogs' eyes and ears come in pairs, or that they have four legs.

2 Create a T-chart on the board or chart paper with the title *Dogs' Legs*. The left column should be titled *Number of Dogs* and the right should be titled *Number of Legs*.

3 Lead the class in filling in the chart. Point out that 1 dog would have 4 legs, 2 dogs would have 8 legs total, 3 dogs would have 12 legs total, 4 dogs would have 16 legs total, and 5 dogs would have 20 legs total. Ask students how they figured that out. Continue the chart through 10 dogs (40 legs).

4 Ask students what other number sets they can identify with the dogs, for example, ears, eyes, or tails. Make another T-chart of number sets with the students. Access students' bodily/kinesthetic intelligence by having them show one of the number patterns with motions. For example, if the pattern increases by two, students might do two jumping jacks, then four jumping jacks, then six jumping jacks, and so on.

5 Tell students that they will be finding number patterns in nature. They will need to collect at least five of one type of item from nature to show to the class (for example, photographs of an animal, leaves, or flowers). As a class, you may brainstorm ideas for nature-collection items or go on a class nature walk for additional ideas.

6 After students have collected their items, distribute copies of the *Patterns in Nature T-Chart* activity sheet (page 60) to students. Have students use this chart to show their pattern extended 10 times. Circulate around the room and assist students, as necessary.

Patterns in Nature

❼ Distribute copies of the *Patterns in Nature Projects* (page 61) to students. Explain that students will select one project to complete and present to the class. Encourage students to select the project that appeals the most to them. Also, students may choose the *interpersonal option* of working with a partner or the *intrapersonal option* of working independently. Provide students with any needed materials to help them complete the activities.

★ **English Language Support**—Give English language learners the opportunity to record their presentation by using audio recorders, so that they can prepare what they want to say and play it for the class.

❽ If you would like to have students collect items and complete the project as homework, distribute copies of the *Patterns in Nature Parent Letter* (page 62) to students. Set a due date for projects and presentations.

❾ If students finish early, they may complete the Anchor Activity.

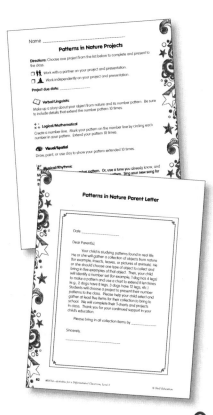

Assessment

Use the *Patterns in Nature Rubric* (page 63) to assess students' work. Keep a record of which projects students selected to assist in planning future multiple-intelligences lessons.

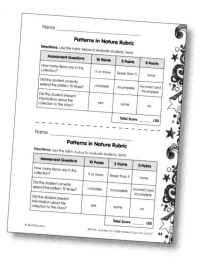

Anchor Activity

Have students make number patterns that follow an addition or subtraction rule. For example, students may pick "add 7." They will take an index card and write five numbers following that rule (e.g., 21, 28, 35, 42, and 49). On the back of the index card, they will write the pattern that their numbers follow. They can trade their number pattern with peers to figure out one another's pattern rule.

Name _____

Patterns in Nature T-Chart

Directions: Use the T-chart below to show a pattern found in nature. Your pattern should repeat at least 10 times.

Title: _____

Number of _____	Number of _____
1	
2	
3	
4	
5	
6	
7	
8	
8	
10	

Name _____

Patterns in Nature Projects

Directions: Choose one project from the list below to complete and present to the class.

❑ 🚶 Work with a partner on your project and presentation.

❑ 🧎 Work independently on your project and presentation.

Project due date: _____

⬜ Verbal/Linguistic

Make up a story about your object from nature and its number pattern. Be sure to include details that extend the number pattern 10 times.

+ − × ÷ Logical/Mathematical

Create a number line. Mark your pattern on the number line by circling each number in your pattern. Extend your pattern 10 times.

👁 Visual/Spatial

Draw, paint, or use clay to show your pattern extended 10 times.

🎵 Musical/Rhythmic

Make up a tune for your number pattern. Or, use a tune you already know, and replace the words with the numbers from your pattern. Sing your new song for the class.

🍂 Naturalist

Take pictures of your object in nature. Print out the pictures and use them to make a poster of your pattern extended 10 times.

Patterns in Nature Parent Letter

Date _____

Dear Parent(s),

Your child is studying patterns found in real life. He or she will gather a collection of objects from nature (for example, insects, leaves, or pictures of animals). He or she should choose one type of object to collect and bring in five examples of that object. Then, your child will identify a number set (for example, 1 dog has 4 legs) to make a pattern and use a chart to extend it ten times (e.g., 2 dogs have 8 legs, 3 dogs have 12 legs, etc.). Students will choose a project to present their number patterns to the class. Please help your child select and gather at least five items for their collection to bring to school. We will complete their T-charts and projects in class. Thank you for your continued support in your child's education.

Please have students bring in all collection items by _____.

Sincerely,

_____

Name _____

Patterns in Nature Rubric

Directions: Use the rubric below to evaluate students' work.

Assessment Questions	10 Points	5 Points	0 Points
How many items are in the collection?	5 or more	fewer than 5	none
Did the student correctly extend the pattern 10 times?	complete	incomplete	incorrect and incomplete
Did the student present information about the collection to the class?	yes	some	no
			Total Score _____ /30

- -

Name _____

Patterns in Nature Rubric

Directions: Use the rubric below to evaluate students' work.

Assessment Questions	10 Points	5 Points	0 Points
How many items are in the collection?	5 or more	fewer than 5	none
Did the student correctly extend the pattern 10 times?	complete	incomplete	incorrect and incomplete
Did the student present information about the collection to the class?	yes	some	no
			Total Score _____ /30

Number Sense

Differentiation Strategy

 Leveled Learning Centers

Standards

- Students will understand symbolic, concrete, and pictorial representations of numbers (e.g., written numerals, objects in sets, number lines).

- TESOL: Students will use English to obtain, process, construct, and provide subject-matter information in spoken and written form.

Materials

- lesson resources (pages 66–69)
- number cubes
- art supplies
- posterboard

Procedures

Preparation Note: Set up three centers in the classroom. Place the following materials at each center:

Center 1—Copies of the *Rolling Number Cubes* activity sheet (page 66), 12 number cubes, pencils

Center 2—Copies of the *ABC Number Line* activity sheet (page 67), copies of the *ABC Number Line Recording Sheet* activity sheet (page 68), pencils

Center 3—Copies of the *Numbers About Me* activity sheet (page 69), pencils; art supplies

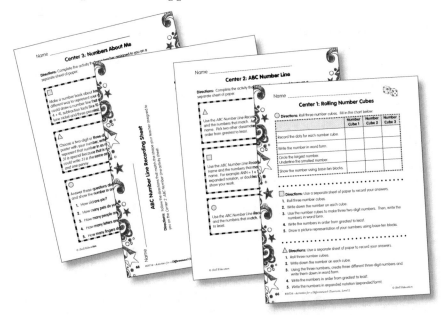

1. Begin by writing the number 17 on the board. Ask students if they know other ways to represent the number 17. If students have a hard time with this, slowly introduce other representations of this number on the board. For example, the number 17 can be shown with base-ten blocks, drawn with tally marks or circles, written in word form (*seventeen*), expanded to 10 + 7, broken apart as 5 + 5 + 7, or represented with coins as one dime, one nickel, and two pennies. Let students share other ways that they could represent the number 17.

2. Tell students that they will be working with numbers and representing them as numerals, pictures, words, and math problems. Each number has a value and it can be shown in different ways.

Number Sense

3 Assign students a shape based on their readiness levels. Tell students to complete the activity next to their assigned shape when they visit each center.

4 Explain the directions for each center and answer any questions that students may have. Assign students to one center to start, or allow them to choose where they would like to begin working.

★ **English Language Support**—Model how to complete each center and partner English language learners with another student at the same readiness level to help explain activities.

5 As students are working, monitor their progress and provide assistance as needed. Once students complete one center, they may move to another center. Or, you may decide to only have students complete one center per day, stretching the activities over a three-day period.

6 If students finish early, they may complete the Anchor Activity.

Assessment

Conduct an informal assessment of student learning by observing students as they work in centers. Take notes to document your observations.

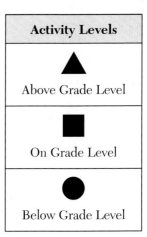

Activity Levels
▲
Above Grade Level
■
On Grade Level
●
Below Grade Level

Anchor Activity

Have students make number riddles. Students will write at least three clues on the front of an index card that describe a number. For example, *I am a three-digit number. I am greater than 100, but I am less than 130. I am odd. When you add up my digits they equal eight. I have a five in the ones place. What number am I?* Students will write the answer for their riddle on the back of their index card. They can share their riddles with their classmates.

Name _____

Center 1: Rolling Number Cubes

○ **Directions:** Roll three number cubes. Fill in the chart below.

	Number Cube 1	Number Cube 2	Number Cube 3
Record the dots for each number cube.			
Write the number in word form.			
Circle the largest number. Underline the smallest number.			
Show the number using base-ten blocks.			

▢ **Directions:** Use a separate sheet of paper to record your answers.

1. Roll three number cubes.
2. Write down the number shown on each cube.
3. Use the number cubes to make three two-digit numbers. Then, write the numbers in word form.
4. Write the numbers in order from greatest to least.
5. Draw a picture representation of your numbers using base-ten blocks.

△ **Directions:** Use a separate sheet of paper to record your answers.

1. Roll three number cubes.
2. Write down the number shown on each cube.
3. Using the three numbers, create three different three-digit numbers and write them down in word form.
4. Write the numbers in order from greatest to least.
5. Write the numbers in expanded notation (expanded form).

Name _____

Center 2: ABC Number Line

Directions: Complete the activity that your teacher assigned to you on a separate sheet of paper.

Use the *ABC Number Line Recording Sheet.* Circle the letters in your name and the numbers that match. Add up all the matching numbers in your name. Pick two other classmates' names to add up. Put your names in order from greatest to least.

Use the *ABC Number Line Recording Sheet.* Circle the letters in your name and the numbers that match. Add up the first three letters in your name. For example ANN = 1 + 14 + 14 = 29. You can use base-ten blocks, expanded notation, or doubles to help you add your letters. Be sure to show your work.

Use the *ABC Number Line Recording Sheet.* Circle the letters in your name and the numbers that match. Put the numbers in order from greatest to least.

Name _____

ABC Number Line Recording Sheet

Directions: Follow the directions that match the shape your teacher assigned to you on the *Center 2: ABC Number Line* activity sheet.

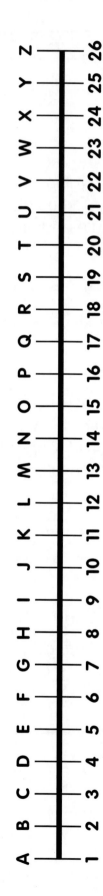

Name _____

Center 3: Numbers About Me

Directions: Complete the activity that your teacher assigned to you on a separate sheet of paper.

Make a number book about how old you are. Each page will have a different way to represent your age. For example, if you are 8 years old, you could draw a number line that shows the number 8, use addition facts (like 4 + 4), subtraction facts (like 10 – 2), base-ten blocks (8 cubes), or money (one nickel and three pennies). Your book should have at least five pages.

Choose a two-digit or three-digit number that is special to you. Make a poster with your number, write why it is special to you, and show how to represent that number in as many different ways as you can. For example, *31 is special because that is my birthday.* Or, *31 = 10 + 10 + 10 + 1.* You could write *31 is the same as thirty-one,* or *31 is also one quarter, one nickel, and one penny.*

Answer these questions about yourself. Write the number in standard form, and show the number in one other way.

1. How old are you?

2. How many pets do you have?

3. How many people are in your family?

4. How many letters are in your name?

5. How many fingers do you have?

Money

Differentiation Strategy

 Menu of Options

Standards

- Students will know processes for telling time, counting money, and measuring length, weight, and temperature, using basic standard and nonstandard units.

- TESOL: Students will use English to obtain, process, construct, and provide subject matter information in spoken and written form.

Materials

- lesson resources (pages 72–75)
- real and plastic coins
- tape
- index cards
- art supplies
- newspaper coupons and advertisements
- clothes hangers
- yarn
- construction paper
- hundred charts (hundred.pdf)
- coin stamps (optional)

Procedures

1 Tell students that they will be creating projects using coins and their values. Ask why they think it is important to learn about coins and their worth. Show a penny, nickel, dime, quarter, half-dollar, and dollar coin. Review the value of each of the coins.

2 Take out several coins and count them with students to find the total value. Have students share other combinations of coins that have the same value. For example, 80 cents could be three quarters and a nickel or a half-dollar and three dimes. Tell students that it is important to know the value of coins and how to make change.

3 Distribute copies of the *Money Menu of Options* activity sheets (pages 72–73) to students and read aloud all of the projects. Explain to students that they will be choosing projects that they want to complete. Model selecting different projects that total 25 points and answer any questions students have. Set a due date for the projects and have students fill it in on their activity sheets.

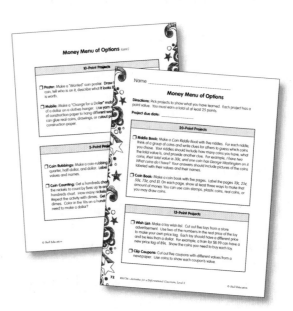

★ **English Language Support**—Tape each type of coin to an index card an label it with its name and value for English language learners to reference.

Money

4 Distribute copies of the *Menu of Options Planning Chart* activity sheet (page 74) to students. Assist students in choosing projects that add up to 25 points. Allow time for students to brainstorm items that they will need to complete their projects. Provide students with any needed materials to help them complete the activities.

5 Provide time for students to work on their projects in class and time to present their projects after they are due.

6 If students finish early, they may complete the Anchor Activity.

Assessment

Have students complete the *Money Menu of Options Student Self-Assessment* (page 75) to evaluate their own learning.

Anchor Activity

Have students create a money activity sheet for the class. Have students create 10 questions for their classmates to solve. They must provide the answers on another sheet of paper. Place these in a mathematics center for others to enjoy. Students can use the answer key to check their own work.

Name _____

Money Menu of Options

Directions: Pick projects to show what you have learned. Each project has a point value. You must earn a total of at least 25 points.

Project due date: _____

20-Point Projects

☐ **Riddle Book:** Make a *Coin Riddle Book* with five riddles. For each riddle, think of a group of coins and write clues for others to guess which coins you chose. Your riddles should include how many coins you have, what the total value is, and provide another clue. For example, *I have two coins, their total value is 30¢, and one coin has George Washington on it. What coins do I have?* Your answers should include pictures of the coins labeled with their values and their names.

☐ **Coin Book:** Make a coin book with five pages. Label the pages *10¢, 25¢, 50¢, 75¢,* and *$1.* On each page, show at least three ways to make that amount of money. You can use coin stamps, plastic coins, real coins, or you may draw coins.

15-Point Projects

☐ **Wish List:** Make a toy wish list. Cut out five toys from a store advertisement. Use two of the numbers in the real price of the toy to make your own price tag. Each toy should have a different price and be less than a dollar. For example, a train for $8.99 can have a new price tag of 89¢. Show the coins you need to buy each toy.

☐ **Clip Coupons:** Cut out five coupons with different values from a newspaper. Use coins to show each coupon's value.

Money Menu of Options *(cont.)*

10-Point Projects

☐ **Poster:** Make a "Wanted" coin poster. Draw the front and back of the coin, tell who is on it, describe what it looks like, and tell what the coin is worth.

☐ **Mobile:** Make a "Change for a Dollar" mobile. Put a large picture of a dollar on a clothes hanger. Use yarn and five different pieces of construction paper to hang different ways to make a dollar. You can glue real coins, drawings, or cutout pictures of coins to the construction paper.

5-Point Projects

☐ **Coin Rubbings:** Make a coin-rubbing collection of a penny, nickel, dime, quarter, half-dollar, and dollar on a large sheet of drawing paper. Label them with the appropriate money values and names.

☐ **Coin Counting:** Get a hundreds chart and a collection of nickels. Use the nickels to count by fives up to one hundred. Color in the 5s on your hundreds chart. How many nickels do you need to make a dollar? Repeat the activity with dimes. Get a hundreds chart and a collection of dimes. Color in the 10s on a hundreds chart. How many dimes do you need to make a dollar?

Name _____

Menu of Options Planning Chart

Directions: Fill in the chart showing what projects you will complete and what items you will need. Return this to your teacher before beginning your work.

Project Name	Points	Items Needed
Project:		
Project:		
Project:		
Due Date: _____	**Total Points:** _____	

Name _____

Money Menu of Options Student Self-Assessment

Directions: Tell about your work by circling *yes* or *no* for each statement.

1. I completed a *Money Menu of Options Planning Chart.*	yes	no
2. I talked with my teacher about my plan.	yes	no
3. I followed directions.	yes	no
4. I completed my projects.	yes	no
5. My projects are neat and organized.	yes	no
6. I can identify a penny, nickel, dime, quarter, half-dollar, and dollar.	yes	no
7. I can add a collection of at least three coins.	yes	no
8. I can show more than one way to make change.	yes	no
9. My projects add up to at least 25 points.	yes	no
10. I did my best.	yes	no
Count the number of circles in the yes column:	_____/10	

Mathematics

Measurement

Differentiation Strategy

 Choices Board

Standards

- Students will understand the basic measures of length, width, height, weight, and temperature.

- TESOL: Students will use English to obtain, process, construct, and provide subject-matter information in spoken and written form.

Materials

- lesson resources (pages 78–81)

- scissors

- paper clips

- cubes

- ruler

- measuring tape

- picture cards of nonstandard units of measure

- textbooks

- toy cars

- marbles

- small balls

- pom-poms

- pocket chart (optional)

Procedures

Preparation Note: Before class begins, make copies of the *Measurement Choices Cards* activity sheets (pages 79–81), cut them apart, and display them on a pocket chart or on a bulletin board.

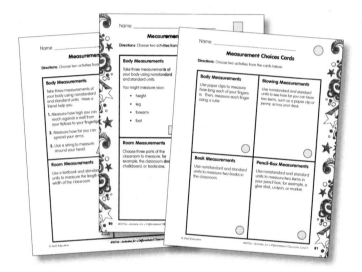

1 Tell students that you want to measure a piece of paper using nonstandard and standard units. See if students understand what that means, and let them make suggestions about standard and nonstandard units. If students have difficulty, choose a nonstandard unit of measurement such as paper clips, cubes, or other items around the classroom. Then, model how you would measure a piece of paper using that nonstandard unit of measure.

2 Allow a volunteer to measure the paper again using another nonstandard unit of measure. Ask students how long the paper is. Be sure to point out the importance of labeling the measurement so that others know which units were used (e.g., 6 *paper clips* or 8 *cubes*).

3 Ask students how papermakers can get all their paper the same length. Tell students that standard units of measurement are the same everywhere. They help people make consistent measurements every time. Let a student measure the piece of paper using a ruler. Have another student measure the paper using a measuring tape. The measurements should be the same.

Measurement

4 Assign students a shape based on their readiness levels.

★ **English Language Support**—Meet in a small group with English language learners to explain directions and help them choose appropriate activities. Have picture cards of nonstandard units of measurement available. Also, if appropriate, address metric measurement and how their home country might use this rather than the American standard.

5 Tell students that they will choose two activities about measurement from a choices board. Point to the *Measurement Choices Cards* (pages 79–81) on your pocket chart or bulletin board. You may also distribute copies of the *Measurement Choices Cards* activity sheets to students based on their readiness levels.

6 Tell students to choose two different activities that match the shape you assigned to them.

7 Distribute copies of the *Measurement Choices Board* activity sheet (page 78) to students. This page can be taken home as homework or used at students' desks so they do not need to consult the class chart. Provide students with any needed materials to help them complete the activities.

8 If students finish early, they may complete the Anchor Activity.

Assessment

Evaluate students' choices board projects to determine whether or not the lesson objectives were met. Plan small-group reteach lessons, as necessary. Make notes on any changes in students' readiness levels for future differentiated lessons on this standard.

Activity Levels
▲
Above Grade Level
■
On Grade Level
●
Below Grade Level

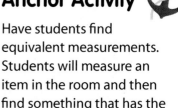

Anchor Activity

Have students find equivalent measurements. Students will measure an item in the room and then find something that has the same measurement. For example, they may measure their foot and then use it to find something that has the same length. Students can share their equivalent measurements with their classmates.

Name _____

Measurement Choices Board

Directions: Choose two activities from the choices below. Make sure your choices match the shape or shapes assigned to you by your teacher.

Path Measurements Use your feet to measure the distance from your desk to another area in the room. Then, measure that distance using a measuring tape.	**Body Measurements** Take three measurements of your body using standard and nonstandard units. You might measure your height, leg, forearm, or foot.	**Pencil-Box Measurements** Use nonstandard and standard units to measure two items in your pencil box, for example, a glue stick, crayon, or marker.
Desk Measurements Choose three items in your desk to measure. Use standard and nonstandard units. You may include your desk as one measurement.	**Blowing Measurements** Use nonstandard and standard units to see how far you can blow two items, such as a paper clip or a penny, across your desk.	**Room Measurements** Use a textbook and standard units to measure the length and width of the classroom.
Body Measurements Use paper clips to measure how long each of your fingers is. Then, measure each finger using a ruler.	**Room Measurements** Choose three parts of the classroom to measure, for example, the classroom door, chalkboard, or bookcase.	**Book Measurements** Use nonstandard and standard units to measure two books in the classroom.
Body Measurements Take three measurements of your body using nonstandard and standard units. Have a friend help you. 1. Measure how high you can reach against a wall from your tiptoes to your fingertips. 2. Measure how far you can spread your arms. 3. Use a string to measure around your head.	**Rolling Measurements** Tilt a textbook off the floor to make a ramp. Use nonstandard and standard units to measure how far a toy car will travel off the ramp. Choose two other items to roll off the ramp and measure, for example, a marble, a ball, or a pom-pom. Put the measurements in order from greatest length to shortest length.	**Moving Measurements** Measure three body movements using standard and nonstandard units. 1. Stand still, then measure the distance you can travel in a single jump. 2. Stand still, then measure the distance you can travel when you hop on one foot. 3. Stand still, then measure how far you can lunge one leg forward.

Name _____

Measurement Choices Cards

Directions: Choose two activities from the cards below.

Body Measurements

Take three measurements of your body using nonstandard and standard units. Have a friend help you.

1. Measure how high you can reach against a wall from your tiptoes to your fingertips.

2. Measure how far you can spread your arms.

3. Use a string to measure around your head.

Rolling Measurements

Tilt a textbook off the floor to make a ramp. Use nonstandard and standard units to measure how far a toy car will travel off the ramp. Choose two other items to roll off the ramp and measure, for example, a marble, a ball, or a pom-pom. Put the measurements in order from greatest length to shortest length.

Room Measurements

Use a textbook and standard units to measure the length and width of the classroom.

Path Measurements

Use your feet to measure the distance from your desk to another area in the room. Then, measure that distance using a measuring tape.

Name _____

Measurement Choices Cards

Directions: Choose two activities from the cards below.

Body Measurements

Take three measurements of your body using nonstandard and standard units.

You might measure your:

- height

- leg

- forearm

- foot

Desk Measurements

Choose three items in your desk to measure. Use standard and nonstandard units. You may include your desk as one measurement.

Room Measurements

Choose three parts of the classroom to measure, for example, the classroom door, chalkboard, or bookcase.

Moving Measurements

Measure three body movements using standard and nonstandard units.

1. Stand still, then measure the distance you can travel in a single jump.

2. Stand still, then measure the distance you can travel when you hop on one foot.

3. Stand still, then measure how far you can lunge one leg forward.

Name _____

Measurement Choices Cards

Directions: Choose two activities from the cards below.

Body Measurements

Use paper clips to measure how long each of your fingers is. Then, measure each finger using a ruler.

Blowing Measurements

Use nonstandard and standard units to see how far you can blow two items, such as a paper clip or penny, across your desk.

Book Measurements

Use nonstandard and standard units to measure two books in the classroom.

Pencil-Box Measurements

Use nonstandard and standard units to measure two items in your pencil box, for example, a glue stick, crayon, or marker.

Shapes

Differentiation Strategy

Tiered Graphic Organizers

Standards

- Students will understand basic properties of (e.g., number of sides, corners, square corners) and similarities and differences between simple geometric shapes.

- TESOL: Students will use English to obtain, process, construct, and provide subject-matter information in spoken and written form.

Materials

- lesson resources (pages 84–87)
- scissors
- construction paper
- paper bag
- chart paper and markers
- picture cards of shapes on index cards

Procedures

Preparation Note: Prior to beginning the lesson, cut out a triangle from construction paper and place it in a paper bag.

❶ Tell students that you have a shape hidden in a bag and that you would like for them to guess the shape. Describe attributes of the shape, including that it is two-dimensional, has three corners, and three sides. Let students guess the shape after each of the attribute clues. Tell students that attributes help us to identify shapes.

❷ Brainstorm a list of two-dimensional (plane) and three-dimensional (solid) shapes with the class on a sheet of chart paper or the board. Ask students which attributes could be used to describe the shapes. The list could include the following:

- bases
- edges
- faces
- sides
- vertices

❸ Tell students that they will be filling out a graphic organizer to show how well they understand shapes and their attributes.

★ **English Language Support**—Have labeled picture cards of shapes available for English language learners. These can be created easily on index cards or on a separate sheet of paper.

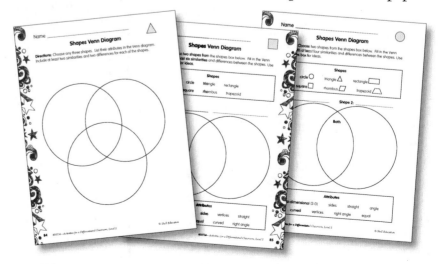

Shapes

4 Assign students a shape based on their readiness levels.

5 Distribute copies of the *Shapes Venn Diagram* activity sheets (pages 84–86) to students based on their readiness levels.

6 Allow students time to complete their Venn diagrams. Then, have students share their graphic organizers with a partner. Tell students that they should explain their graphic organizers to their partners.

7 If students finish early, they may complete the Anchor Activity.

Assessment

Have students use the *Shapes Venn Diagram Partner-Assessment* (page 87) to evaluate their partner's work.

Activity Levels
▲
Above Grade Level
■
On Grade Level
●
Below Grade Level

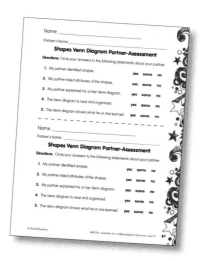

Anchor Activity

Have students create models of two-dimensional (2-D) and three-dimensional (3-D) shapes using items in the classroom, and provide a real-world example of that shape. For example, students can make an octagon out of craft sticks and then draw a stop sign next to the octagon. Have students display their models in the classroom.

Name _____

Shapes Venn Diagram

Directions: Choose any three shapes. List their attributes in the Venn diagram. Include at least two similarities and two differences for each of the shapes.

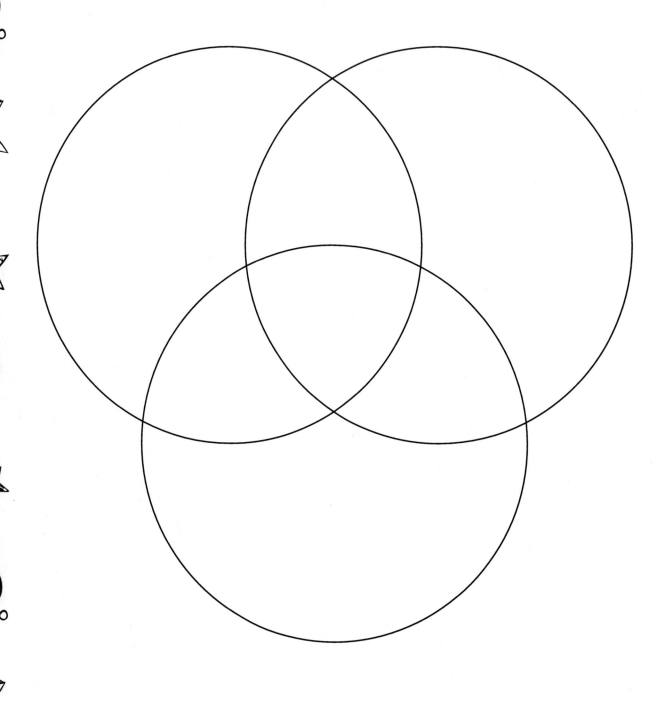

Name _____

Shapes Venn Diagram

Directions: Choose two shapes from the Shapes box below. Fill in the Venn diagram with at least six similarities and differences between the shapes. Use the Attributes box for ideas.

Shapes		
circle	triangle	rectangle
square	rhombus	trapezoid

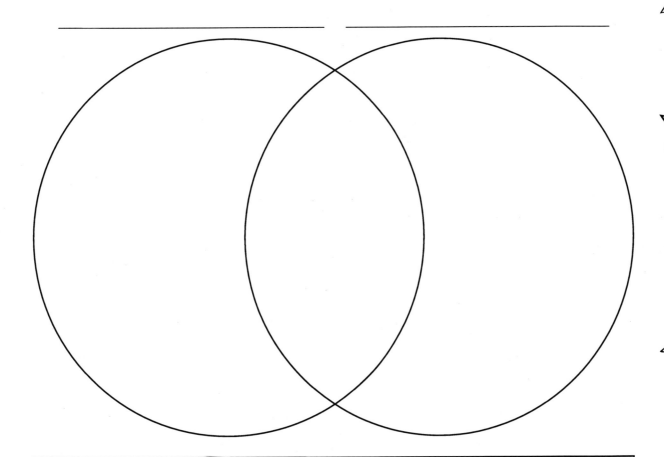

Attributes			
two-dimensional (2-D)	sides	vertices	straight
angle parallel	equal	curved	right angle

Name _____

Shapes Venn Diagram

Directions: Choose two shapes from the Shapes box below. Fill in the Venn diagram with at least four similarities and differences between the shapes. Use the Attributes box for ideas.

Shapes

circle ○   triangle △   rectangle ▭

square ☐   rhombus ▱   trapezoid ⏢

Shape 1: _____   **Shape 2:** _____

Both

Attributes

two-dimensional (2-D)   sides   straight   angle

curved   vertices   right angle   equal

#50734—*Activities for a Differentiated Classroom, Level 2*

Name _____

Partner's Name _____

Shapes Venn Diagram Partner-Assessment

Directions: Circle your answers to the following statements about your partner.

1. My partner identified shapes.   **yes**   some   **no**

2. My partner listed attributes of the shapes.   **yes**   some   **no**

3. My partner explained his or her Venn diagram.   **yes**   some   **no**

4. The Venn diagram is neat and organized.   **yes**   some   **no**

5. The Venn diagram shows what he or she learned.   **yes**   some   **no**

– –

Name _____

Partner's Name _____

Shapes Venn Diagram Partner-Assessment

Directions: Circle your answers to the following statements about your partner.

1. My partner identified shapes.   **yes**   some   **no**

2. My partner listed attributes of the shapes.   **yes**   some   **no**

3. My partner explained his or her Venn diagram.   **yes**   some   **no**

4. The Venn diagram is neat and organized.   **yes**   some   **no**

5. The Venn diagram shows what he or she learned.   **yes**   some   **no**

Fractions

Differentiation Strategy

 Tiered Assignments

Standards

• Students will understand the concept of a unit and its subdivision into equal parts, for example, a whole pizza versus slices of the whole to make fractions.

• TESOL: Students will use English to obtain, process, construct, and provide subject-matter information in spoken and written form.

Materials

• lesson resources (pages 90–93)

• sets of pattern blocks: 1 hexagon, 2 trapezoids, 3 rhombuses, and 6 triangles

• one-inch grid paper

• art supplies

Procedures

1 Tell students that they will learn about fractions. Distribute sets of pattern blocks with one hexagon, two trapezoids, three rhombuses, and six triangles to each student.

2 Ask students to take out a hexagon. The hexagon will represent the *whole* shape amount in this lesson. Have students trace the hexagon on a sheet of drawing paper and label it *one whole*.

3 Ask students what shape they would have if they cut the hexagon into two equal parts. What would half of a hexagon look like? Students can cover their hexagon with two trapezoids to see that two trapezoids would make a hexagon. Have students trace the trapezoids in the shape of a hexagon, color one trapezoid, and label it as $\frac{1}{2}$.

4 Ask students what shape they would have if they cut the hexagon into three equal parts. What would one-third of a hexagon look like? The students can cover their hexagon with three rhombuses. Have students trace the three rhombuses, shade two, and label that part as $\frac{2}{3}$. Explain that since two of the three parts are colored, it represents two-thirds of the whole hexagon.

5 Ask students what shape they would have if they cut the hexagon into six equal parts. What would one-sixth of a hexagon look like? Students can cover their hexagons with six triangles. Have students trace the triangles in the shape of a hexagon, and choose a fraction (such as $\frac{1}{6}$) for them to shade and label. Continue to model a variety of fractions with students.

6 Tell students that they will be working on fractions with food. Distribute copies of the *Chocolate Bar Fractions* activity sheet (page 90) and the *Pizza Slices and Toppings Fractions* activity sheets (pages 91–92) to students based on their readiness levels. Provide students with any needed materials to help them complete the activities.

★ **English Language Support**—English language leaners can be at all levels academically. Assign them the appropriate activity sheet and partner these students with language-proficient students. Meet with your English language learners who are below grade level to work with them in a small group.

Activity Levels
▲
Above Grade Level
■
On Grade Level
●
Below Grade Level

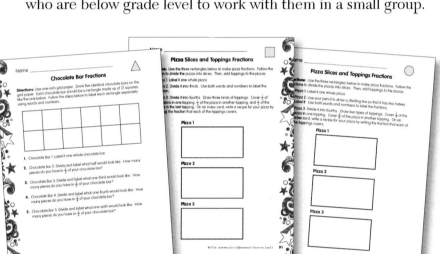

7 If students finish early, they may complete the Anchor Activity.

Assessment

To assess what students have learned, use the *Fractions Rubric* (page 93) for each student. There is one rubric for the circle and square activities and a different rubric for the triangle activity.

Anchor Activity

Have students create fractions using spinners. Provide students with four-quadrant spinners labeled 1, 2, 3, and 4. Students will spin twice and use those numbers to make a fraction and model that fraction using snap cubes. For example, if a student spins a 1 and 4, his or her fraction would be one-fourth or $\frac{1}{4}$. The student could take one pink snap cube and three blue snap cubes to show $\frac{1}{4}$. Students will write their fraction on a sticky note and place it by their models.

Name _____

Chocolate Bar Fractions

Directions: Use one-inch grid paper. Draw five identical chocolate bars on the grid paper. Each chocolate bar should be a rectangle made up of 12 squares, like the one shown below. Follow the steps below to label each rectangle separately using words and numbers.

1. Chocolate Bar 1: Label it one whole chocolate bar.

2. Chocolate Bar 2: Divide and label what half would look like. How many pieces do you have in $\frac{1}{2}$ of your chocolate bar?

3. Chocolate Bar 3: Divide and label what one-third would look like. How many pieces do you have in $\frac{1}{3}$ of your chocolate bar?

4. Chocolate Bar 4: Divide and label what one-fourth would look like. How many pieces do you have in $\frac{1}{4}$ of your chocolate bar?

5. Chocolate Bar 5: Divide and label what one-sixth would look like. How many pieces do you have in $\frac{1}{6}$ of your chocolate bar?

Name _____

Pizza Slices and Toppings Fractions

Directions: Use the three rectangles below to make pizza fractions. Follow the directions to divide the pizzas into slices. Then, add toppings to the pizzas.

1. Pizza 1: Label it one whole pizza.

2. Pizza 2: Divide it into thirds. Use both words and numbers to label the fraction.

3. Pizza 3: Divide it into fourths. Draw three kinds of toppings. Cover $\frac{1}{4}$ of the pizza in one topping, $\frac{1}{4}$ of the pizza in another topping, and $\frac{2}{4}$ of the pizza in the last topping. On an index card, write a recipe for your pizza by writing the fraction that each of the toppings covers.

Pizza 1

Pizza 2

Pizza 3

Name _____

Pizza Slices and Toppings Fractions

Directions: Use the three rectangles below to make pizza fractions. Follow the directions to divide the pizzas into slices. Then, add toppings to the pizzas.

1. Pizza 1: Label it one whole pizza.

2. Pizza 2: Use your pencil to draw a dividing line so that it has two halves. Label it. Use both words and numbers to label the fractions.

3. Pizza 3: Divide it into fourths. Draw two types of toppings. Cover $\frac{1}{4}$ of the pizza in one topping. Cover $\frac{3}{4}$ of the pizza in another topping. On an index card, write a recipe for your pizza by writing the fraction that each of the toppings covers.

Pizza 1

Pizza 2

Pizza 3

Student: _____

△ Fractions Rubric

Teacher Directions: Use the rubric below for the *Chocolate Bar Fractions* activity sheets.

Criteria	Poor	Needs Work	Fair	Strong	Outstanding
The student labeled the fractions using words and numbers.	1	2	3	4	5
The student correctly identified and labeled the number of pieces in one-half.	1	2	3	4	5
The student correctly identified and labeled the number of pieces in one-third.	1	2	3	4	5
The student correctly identified and labeled the number of pieces in one-fourth.	1	2	3	4	5
The student correctly identified and labeled the number of pieces in one-sixth.	1	2	3	4	5

Teacher Comments:

Points: _____ **/ 25**

– –

Student: _____

◯ ▢ Fractions Rubric

Teacher Directions: Use the rubric below for the *Pizza Slices and Toppings Fractions* activity sheets.

Criteria	Poor	Needs Work	Fair	Strong	Outstanding
The student labeled the fractions using words and numbers.	1	2	3	4	5
The student correctly divided the pizza into equal parts.	1	2	3	4	5
The student added the correct number of toppings.	1	2	3	4	5
The student covered the correct fraction of each pizza with toppings.	1	2	3	4	5
The student's recipe card is correct.	1	2	3	4	5

Teacher Comments:

Points: _____ **/ 25**

Science

Earth, Moon, and Sun

Differentiation Strategy

 Menu of Options

Standards

- Students know basic patterns of the sun and moon.

- TESOL: Students will use English to obtain, process, construct, and provide subject matter information in spoken and written form.

Materials

- lesson resources (pages 96–99)

- flashlight

- sign labeled *Earth*

- audio recorder *(optional)*

Procedures

Note: This lesson is an appropriate culmination for a unit of study on Earth, the moon, and the sun. This lesson is intended to take multiple days.

1 Review with students that the sun is the star at the center of our solar system, and that Earth and other planets orbit the sun. Have a student stand in the middle of the room with a flashlight to represent the sun.

2 Choose a student to represent Earth. Give him or her a sign labeled *Earth*, and have the student walk slowly around the student representing the sun.

3 Ask students the following questions:

- How long will it take Earth to orbit the sun? (*one year or 365 days*) Then, ask the "Earth" student to slowly turn his or her body in a complete revolution while he or she is slowly walking around the sun.

- How long does it take for Earth to rotate around its axis? (*one day or 24 hours*)

- Identify which side of "Earth" is day and which side is night.

4 Choose a student to represent the moon. Have him or her walk around "Earth." Ask how long it takes for the moon to orbit Earth. (*about 28 days or one month*)

5 Distribute copies of the *Earth, Moon, and Sun Menu of Options* activity sheet (page 96) to students and read through the projects aloud. Answer any questions that students may have.

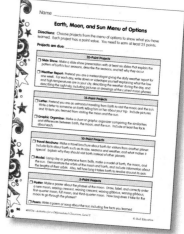

Earth, Moon, and Sun

6 Distribute copies of the *Menu of Options Planning Chart* activity sheet (page 97) to students and allow them time to discuss which projects they want to do. Explain to students that they must choose several projects that total 25 points or more. Model for students how they might select different options that total 25 points.

★ **English Language Support**—Make language-friendly project modifications for English language learners, such as having students verbally explain their facts to you or make an audio recording of their facts.

7 Students may take their menus and planning charts home along with the *Earth, Moon, and Sun Parent Letter* (page 98) to discuss project options with their parents. Have students fill out the chart and return it to class.

8 Have students work on their projects at home over a week. When projects are due, allow time for students to share one or more of the projects that they completed.

9 Students may complete the Anchor Activity as an extra-credit option.

Assessment

Before the projects are due, send home the *Earth, Moon, and Sun Parent and Student Assessment* (page 99) and have students work with their parents to complete the assessment of their work.

Anchor Activity

Have students make constellation mobiles. Students can research a constellation, draw it, and hang constellation facts from their mobiles.

Name _____

Earth, Moon, and Sun Menu of Options

Directions: Choose projects from the menu of options to show what you have learned. Each project has a point value. You need to earn at least 25 points.

Projects are due: _____

20-Point Projects

☐ **Slide Show:** Make a slide show presentation with at least six slides that explain the pattern of Earth's four seasons, describe the seasons, and tell why they occur.

☐ **Weather Report:** Pretend you are a meteorologist giving the daily weather report for one week. For each day, write down or videotape yourself explaining what the low and high temperatures are in your city, describing the weather during the day, and describing the night sky. Include pictures or drawings of the current moon phases.

15-Point Projects

☐ **Letter:** Pretend you are an astronaut traveling from Earth to visit the moon and the sun. Write a letter to someone on Earth telling him or her about your trip. Include pictures and 10 facts that you learned from visiting the moon and the sun.

☐ **Graphic Organizer:** Make a chart or graphic organizer comparing the similarities and differences between Earth, the moon, and the sun. Include at least five facts about each.

10-Point Projects

☐ **Travel Brochure:** Make a travel brochure about Earth for visitors from another planet. Include facts about Earth such as its size, seasons and weather, and what makes it special. Explain why they should visit Earth instead of other planets.

☐ **Model:** Using clay or polystyrene foam balls, make a model of Earth, the moon, and the sun. Demonstrate the orbits of the moon and Earth, and include information about the lengths of their orbits. Also, tell how long it takes Earth to revolve around its axis.

5-Point Projects

☐ **Poster:** Make a poster about the phases of the moon. Draw, label, and correctly order a new moon, waxing crescent, waning crescent, waxing gibbous, waning gibbous, first-quarter moon, full moon, and third-quarter moon. How long does it take for the moon to go through the phases?

☐ **Poem:** Write a poem or song about the sun that includes five facts you have learned.

Name _____

Menu of Options Planning Chart

Directions: Fill in the chart showing what projects you will complete and what items you will need. Return this to your teacher before beginning your work.

Project Name	Points	Items Needed
Project:		
Project:		
Project:		
Due Date: _____	Total Points: _____	

Earth, Moon, and Sun Parent Letter

Date _____

Dear Parent(s),

Your child has been learning about Earth, the moon, and the sun in class. He or she is bringing home an *Earth, Moon, and Sun Menu of Options* and *Menu of Options Planning Chart*. Please look over the various project options and help your child choose activities to complete. Each project has a point value. Choose projects that will total at least 25 points.

Help your child complete the *Earth, Moon, and Sun Menu of Options Planning Chart* and have your child return it to class. Your child will need to work on his or her projects at home.

Before the projects are due, your child will bring home an assessment titled *Earth, Moon, and Sun Parent and Student Assessment*. Please work with your child to evaluate his or her work, complete the assessment, and return it to class.

All projects are due: _____.

Thank you for your continued support.

Sincerely,

_____

Name _____

Earth, Moon, and Sun
Parent and Student Assessment

Directions: Circle or color the face that shows the answer to each statement.

1. I showed what I know about Earth, the moon, and the sun.	☺ 😐 ☹
2. I completed projects that total at least 25 points.	☺ 😐 ☹
3. My projects are neat.	☺ 😐 ☹
4. I followed directions in completing projects.	☺ 😐 ☹
5. The information in my projects is correct.	☺ 😐 ☹

Parent Comments:

_____

_____

_____

Water Cycle

Differentiation Strategy

 Leveled Learning Centers

Standards

- Students will know that water can be a liquid or a solid and can be made to change from one form to the other while the amount of water stays the same.

- TESOL: Students will use English to obtain, process, construct, and provide subject-matter information in spoken and written form.

Materials

- lesson resources (pages 102–105)
- construction paper
- art supplies
- cotton balls
- tissue paper
- measuring cup
- water
- microwave
- cold can or bottle of water or juice

Procedures

Preparation Note: Prepare three centers in the classroom. Place copies of the *Water Cycle Centers* activity sheets (pages 103–105) at the appropriate center, along with paper and pencils. Center 1 also requires construction paper and art supplies. This lesson can be spread out over several days.

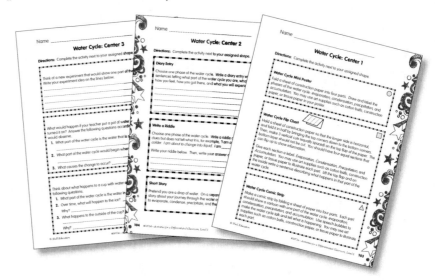

1 Ask students where they think rain comes from. Tell them that the amount of water on Earth does not change, but water changes form—from solid ice, to liquid water, to vapor. The water cycle shows how water moves above, below, and on Earth's surface. Display the *Water Cycle Example* activity sheet (page 102) and distribute copies to students. Point out where *evaporation*, *condensation*, *precipitation*, and *accumulation* occur on their sheets. Have students label these parts on the activity sheet during the lesson. Use this for review and as a visual for English language learners.

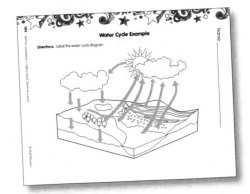

2 To demonstrate the concept of *evaporation*, heat a measuring cup of water in a microwave for two minutes. It should be at the boiling point. Let students see the steam rising from the measuring cup. Ask students to explain what is happening. They should state that when a liquid is heated, it turns into a gas. If the cup continued to be heated for a long time, all of the water would eventually evaporate (change from liquid form to gas).

3 To demonstrate the concept of *condensation*, bring in a very cold can of juice or a glass of ice water. Have students observe the outside of the can or glass to see water drops forming. Ask students where this water came from. Explain that water exists in the air all around us as a gas. The cold liquid inside the can or glass cooled the air surrounding it. When water vapor in the air cools, it changes from a gas to a liquid, which is called condensation. When condensation occurs in the sky, the drops of water stick to dust and form clouds.

4 To demonstrate the concept of *precipitation*, hold up the juice can or glass of water and let the liquid drip down. Students can see that when water vapor in the sky is cooled from a gas to a liquid, it falls to Earth as rain (in liquid form) or hail (in solid form). Explain that *accumulation* is the term for all the water that collects on Earth's surface in rivers, lakes, or oceans. On the board, illustrate how snow on mountaintops melts and flows into rivers and eventually ends up in the ocean.

5 Assign students a shape based on their readiness levels. Go over the directions for each of the centers and answer any questions students have. Assign students to different centers.

★ **English Language Support**—Visit the centers where English language learners are working and be available to guide them through the activities.

6 As students are working, monitor their progress and scaffold, as needed. Have students rotate through all of the centers.

7 If students finish early, they may complete the Anchor Activity.

Assessment

Observe and take anecdotal notes as students work at centers.

Activity Levels
▲
Above Grade Level
■
On Grade Level
●
Below Grade Level

Anchor Activity

Have students write an acrostic poem on the water cycle using the letters in "water cycle." Encourage students to use the vocabulary terms that they have learned, such as *evaporation*, *condensation*, *precipitation*, and *accumulation*. Display the students' poems in the classroom and let them read their acrostics to their peers.

Name _____

Water Cycle Example

Directions: Label the water cycle diagram.

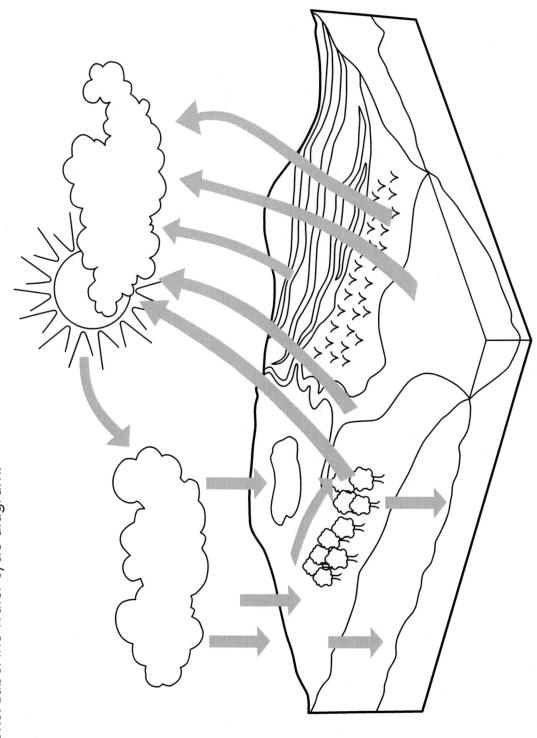

Name _____

Water Cycle: Center 1

Directions: Complete the activity next to your assigned shape.

Water Cycle Mini Poster

Fold a sheet of construction paper into four parts. Draw and label the phases of the water cycle: *evaporation, condensation, precipitation*, and *accumulation*. You may use art supplies such as cotton balls, construction paper, or tissue paper in your poster.

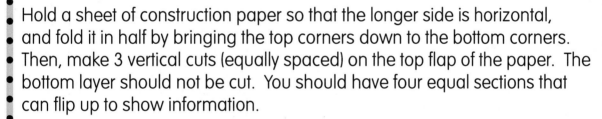

Water Cycle Flip Chart

Hold a sheet of construction paper so that the longer side is horizontal, and fold it in half by bringing the top corners down to the bottom corners. Then, make 3 vertical cuts (equally spaced) on the top flap of the paper. The bottom layer should not be cut. You should have four equal sections that can flip up to show information.

Give each section a label: *Evaporation, Condensation, Precipitation*, and *Accumulation*. You may use art supplies such as cotton balls, construction paper, or tissue paper to illustrate each part. Lift the top flap and on the inside write a sentence describing what happens in that part of the water cycle.

Water Cycle Comic Strip

Make a comic strip by folding a sheet of paper into four parts. Each part should show a cartoon with one part of the water cycle: *evaporation, condensation, precipitation*, and *accumulation*. Use speech bubbles to make the water cycle talk and tell what is happening. You may use art supplies such as cotton balls, construction paper, or tissue paper to illustrate each part.

Name _____

Water Cycle: Center 2

Directions: Complete the activity next to your assigned shape.

Diary Entry

Choose one phase of the water cycle. Write a diary entry with at least five sentences telling what part of the water cycle you are, what you look like, how you feel, how you got there, and what you will experience next.

_____

_____

_____

_____

_____

Write a Riddle

Choose one phase of the water cycle. Write a riddle about it. A riddle gives clues but does not tell what it is, for example, _"I am a cloud that is getting colder. I am about to change into liquid. I am _____."_

Write your riddle below. Then, write your answer on the back of this sheet.

_____

_____

_____

Short Story

Pretend that you are a drop of water. On a separate sheet of paper, write a short story about your journey through the water cycle. Describe what it was like to evaporate, condense, precipitate, and then accumulate.

Name _____

Water Cycle: Center 3

Directions: Complete the activity next to your assigned shape.

△

Think of a new experiment that would show one part of the water cycle. Write your experiment idea on the lines below.

_____
_____
_____
_____

▢

What would happen if your teacher put a pot of water on a stove and turned it on? Answer the following questions according to what you would observe.

1. What part of the water cycle is the water that is sitting in a pot?

   _____

2. What part of the water cycle would begin when the stove is turned on?

   _____

3. What causes the change to occur? _____

◯

Think about what happens to a cup with water and ice in it. Answer the following questions.

1. What part of the water cycle is the water in the cup? _____

2. Over time, what will happen to the ice? _____

   Why? _____

3. What happens to the outside of the cup?

   _____

   Why? _____

Properties of Matter

Differentiation Strategy

 Choices Board

Standards

- Students will know that different objects are made up of many different types of materials and have many different observable properties.

- TESOL: Students will use English to obtain, process, construct, and provide subject-matter information in spoken and written form.

Materials

- lesson resources (pages 108–111)

- an orange

- dry pancake mix, water, mixing bowl, and spoon

- electric griddle and spatula

- measuring cups and spoons

- *choices board materials:* glue, ice cubes, snap cubes, blow-dryer, construction paper, baking soda, vinegar, balance scale, antacid tablets, cups, water

Procedures

1 Review the different properties of matter by showing students an orange. Ask students to describe it to you without saying that it is an orange. Record students' responses on a sheet of chart paper or the board. Remind students that people describe objects using size, shape, weight, color, and textures. These are the properties of the object. The properties show how the object looks, feels, or acts.

2 Demonstrate properties of matter and how temperature can make those properties change. Begin by showing students a bowl of dry pancake mix and asking them to describe some of its properties. Is it as a solid, liquid, or gas? What is its color and texture?

3 Measure water according to the directions on the pancake mix box, and ask students to describe some properties of water. Is it a solid, liquid, or gas? Does it have its own shape? Add the water to the dry pancake mix and stir to create the batter. What changes occur? Describe how the properties changed.

4 Ask students how they can change the liquid batter back to a solid. Warm up an electric griddle. Pour the batter on the griddle and let students observe the changes that occur. What is happening to the liquid batter? What state of matter are the bubbles? What change caused the liquid to turn into a solid? Students should understand that it is the temperature that caused the properties to change.

5 Tell students that they will be choosing two activities about properties of matter from the class choices board. Assign students a shape based on their readiness levels.

6 Cut apart and display the *Properties of Matter Choices Cards* activity sheets (pages 109–111) on a hanging chart or bulletin board. (A blank square is available on each page so that you can add an additional activity. Students can also suggest an alternative activity.) Or, distribute copies of the *Properties of Matter Choices Board* (page 108) so that each student can have his or her own copy.

7 Let students choose two activities to complete that match the shape assigned to them.

★ **English Language Support**—Find objects around the classroom that provide examples of important words that describe properties of matter (e.g., smooth, rough, soft, hard).

8 If students finish early, they may complete the Anchor Activity.

Activity Levels
Above Grade Level
On Grade Level
Below Grade Level |

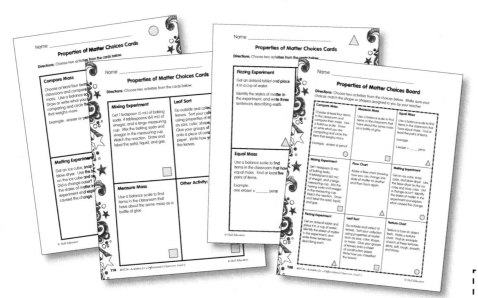

Assessment

Circulate and ask questions of students as they work to make sure that they are staying on task and understanding the concepts being taught. Record notes of your informal assessment of students' comprehension.

Anchor Activity

Have students invent a new object (such as a toy or food) and write an advertisement for it. The object can be a solid, liquid, or gas. Students should describe what the object can do and how it changes from one state of matter to another. They should include an illustration in the advertisement.

Name _____

Properties of Matter Choices Board

Directions: Choose two activities from the choices below. Make sure your choices match the shape or shapes assigned to you by your teacher.

Compare Mass	**Measure Mass**	**Equal Mass**
Choose at least four items in the classroom and compare their mass. Use a balance scale. Draw or write what you are comparing and circle the item that weighs more. **Example:** eraser or pencil	Use a balance scale to find items in the classroom that have about the same mass as a bottle of glue.	Use a balance scale to find items in the classroom that have equal mass. Find at least five pairs of items. **Example:** 1 eraser = _____ pens
Mixing Experiment	**Flow Chart**	**Melting Experiment**
Get 1 teaspoon (5 mL) of baking soda, 4 tablespoons (60 mL) of vinegar, and a large measuring cup. Mix the baking soda and vinegar in the measuring cup. Watch the reaction. Draw and label the solid, liquid, and gas.	Make a flow chart showing how you can change one state of matter to another and then back again.	Get an ice cube, snap cube, and blow-dryer. Use the blow-dryer on the ice cube and snap cube. Did a change occur? Identify the states of matter in the experiment and explain what caused the change.
Fizzing Experiment	**Leaf Sort**	**Texture Chart**
Get an antacid tablet and place it in a cup of water. Identify the tablet's states of matter in the experiment, and write three sentences describing each.	Go outside and collect 10 leaves. Sort your collection using properties of matter such as size, color, shape, or mass. Glue your groups of leaves onto a sheet of construction paper. Write how you classified the leaves.	Texture is how an object feels. Make a texture chart. Find an example of each of these textures: sticky, soft, rough, smooth, and sharp.

 #50734—*Activities for a Differentiated Classroom, Level 2*

Name _____

Properties of Matter Choices Cards

Directions: Choose two activities from the cards below.

Fizzing Experiment

Get an antacid tablet and place it in a cup of water.

Identify the tablet's states of matter in the experiment, and write three sentences describing each.

Flow Chart

Make a flow chart showing how you can change one state of matter to another and then back again.

Equal Mass

Use a balance scale to find items in the classroom that have equal mass. Find at least five pairs of items.

Example:
1 eraser = _____ pens

Other Activity:

Name _____

Properties of Matter Choices Cards

Directions: Choose two activities from the cards below.

Mixing Experiment

Get 1 teaspoon (5 mL) of baking soda, 4 tablespoons (60 mL) of vinegar, and a large measuring cup. Mix the baking soda and vinegar in the measuring cup. Watch the reaction. Draw and label the solid, liquid, and gas.

Leaf Sort

Go outside and collect 10 leaves. Sort your collection using properties of matter such as size, color, shape, or mass. Glue your groups of leaves onto a piece of construction paper. Write how you classified the leaves.

Measure Mass

Use a balance scale to find items in the classroom that have about the same mass as a bottle of glue.

Other Activity:

Name _____

Properties of Matter Choices Cards

Directions: Choose two activities from the cards below.

Compare Mass

Choose at least four items in the classroom and compare their mass. Use a balance scale. Draw or write what you are comparing and circle the item that weighs more.

Example: eraser or pencil

Texture Chart

Texture is how an object feels. Make a texture chart. Find an example of each of these textures: sticky, soft, rough, smooth, and sharp.

Melting Experiment

Get an ice cube, snap cube, and blow-dryer. Use the blow-dryer on the ice cube and snap cube. Did a change occur? Identify the states of matter in the experiment and explain what caused the change.

Other Activity:

Animals

Differentiation Strategy

Tiered Graphic Organizers

Standards

- Students will know that there are similarities and differences in the appearance and behavior of plants and animals.

- TESOL: Students will use English to obtain, process, construct, and provide subject-matter information in spoken and written form.

Materials

- lesson resources (pages 114–117)

- one live animal or animal photo or video for observation

- chart paper and markers

- books and websites about animals

Procedures

Preparation Note: If possible, bring in a live animal for students to study (e.g., a fish, turtle, hamster). Some students might have a small pet that they could bring in for the day. If this is not possible, bring in a picture or show a video of an animal.

1 Tell students that all animals have characteristics that make them distinct and help them to survive. Have students observe the physical characteristics of the animal, and create a list as a whole group of the animal's body parts and body covering.

2 Ask students to identify any special adaptations that the animal has to help it survive. For example, a fish has gills to help it breathe under water. A turtle has webbed feet to swim. Next, ask students to identify the habitat where the animal lives and its basic needs for survival (e.g., food, water, shelter). Ask students to discuss how the animal meets its needs in its environment.

3 Draw a tree diagram on the board or a sheet of chart paper and label it *Animal Kingdom*. Tell students that animals belong to different classifications within the animal kingdom. Scientists classify animals in the animal kingdom first by whether the animal has a backbone (vertebrate) or does not have a backbone (invertebrate). Draw two branches on the tree diagram, and label one *Vertebrates* and the other *Invertebrates*. For example, a dog is a vertebrate and a jellyfish is an invertebrate. Ask students to classify the animal that the class is studying as a vertebrate or an invertebrate.

4 Explain that vertebrates are classified into the following categories: mammals, reptiles, birds, fish, and amphibians. Add a branch for each of these five categories to your tree diagram on the board. Discuss and list some of the basic features of each of these types of animals, and brainstorm examples as a class. Characteristics include the following:

> **Mammals:** warm-blooded, hair, most have live babies that are fed milk by their mothers
>
> **Birds:** warm-blooded, wings, feathers, most can fly, lay eggs
>
> **Reptiles:** cold-blooded, scaly skin, lay eggs
>
> **Fish:** cold-blooded, live in the water, use gills to breathe, lay eggs
>
> **Amphibians:** cold-blooded, lay eggs, soft/moist skin, live in water and on land

5 Tell students that they will be studying an animal of their choice and making a web to organize all their information.

★ **English Language Support**—Have English language learners draw pictures and orally explain their webs. Help students to create a word bank to assist them with their writing.

6 Distribute copies of the *Animal Web* activity sheets (pages 114–116) to students based on their readiness levels. Provide students with books or access to websites about animals to help them with their research. Once students have completed their graphic organizers, have them share their work with a partner.

Activity Levels
▲
Above Grade Level
■
On Grade Level
●
Below Grade Level

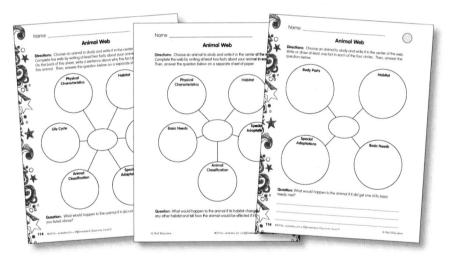

7 If students finish early, they may complete the Anchor Activity.

Assessment

As students are sharing their graphic organizers with their partners, circulate around the room and listen to students' explanations. Use the *Animal Assessment Checklist* (page 117) to keep track of student progress.

Anchor Activity

Have students choose one classification of vertebrates. Ask students to brainstorm animals that fall into that classification. They can ask their peers to guess which classification they chose by looking at their list.

Name _____

Animal Web

Directions: Choose an animal to study and write it in the center of the web. Complete the web by writing at least two facts about your animal in each circle. On the back of this sheet, write a sentence about why this fact is important to this animal. Then, answer the question below on a separate sheet of paper.

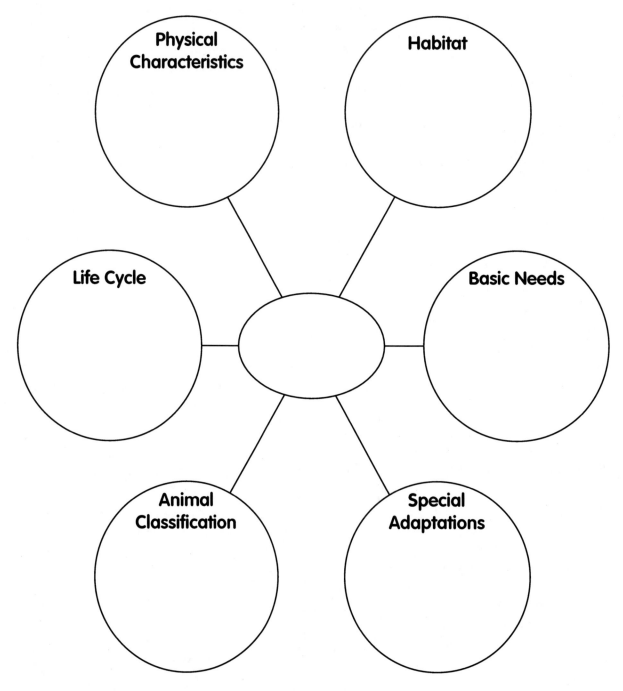

Physical Characteristics

Habitat

Life Cycle

Basic Needs

Animal Classification

Special Adaptations

Question: What would happen to the animal if it did not have the adaptations you listed above?

Name _____

Animal Web

Directions: Choose an animal to study and write it in the center of the web. Complete the web by writing at least two facts about your animal in each circle. Then, answer the question below on a separate sheet of paper.

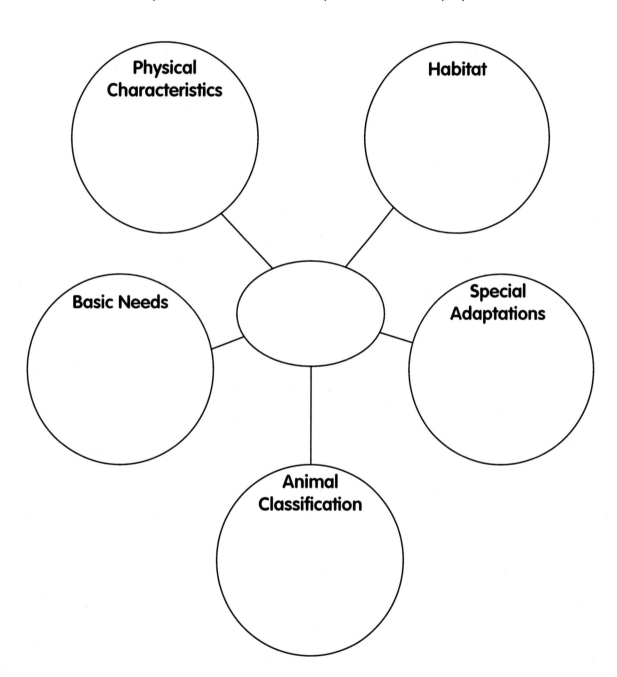

Physical Characteristics

Habitat

Basic Needs

Special Adaptations

Animal Classification

Question: What would happen to the animal if its habitat changed? Choose any other habitat and tell how the animal would be affected if it lived there.

Name _____

Animal Web

Directions: Choose an animal to study and write it in the center of the web. Write or draw at least one fact in each of the four circles. Then, answer the question below.

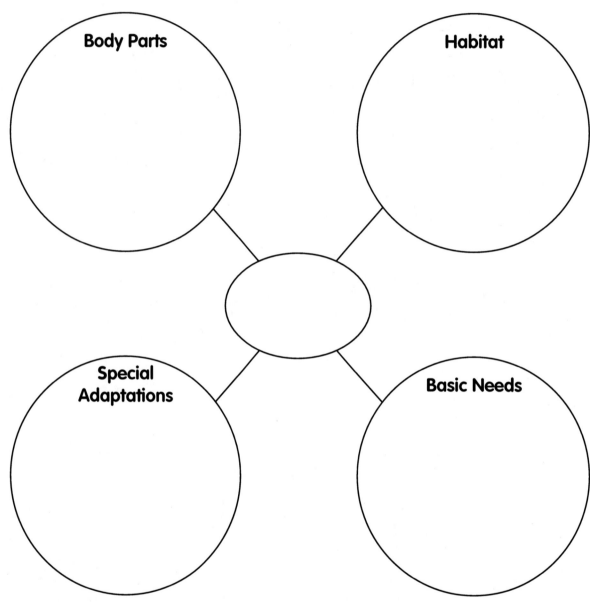

Question: What would happen to the animal if it did get one of its basic needs met?

_____

_____

Animal Assessment Checklist

Teacher Directions: Use the checklist below to assess students' performance. Use checkmarks (✔) in the criteria columns to indicate proficiency.

Student Name	Lists characteristics	Identifies basic needs	Knows the habitat	Understands adaptations

Parts of a Plant

Differentiation Strategy

 Multiple Intelligences

Standards

- Students know that plants and animals have features that help them to live in different environments.

- TESOL: Students will use English to obtain, process, construct, and provide subject-matter information in spoken and written form.

Materials

- lesson resources (pages 120–123)
- plant seeds
- plant
- pictures of plants from different habitats
- books or websites about different plants

Procedures

Preparation Note: Schedule time in the school library or computer lab for students to research plants. This lesson will take multiple days.

1 Begin by showing students some plant seeds. Let students touch the seeds. Then show students a plant. Ask students to turn to partners and explain how the seed turned into a plant. Some students might know, but others will not know. Tell students that the class is going to find out how this happens.

2 Remind students that in your classroom, all students have a job to do to make your classroom run smoothly. Some students hold the door open, others take the lunch count, and some are the line leaders. Tell students that in the same way, each part of a plant has a special job or function. Display pictures of plants from different habitats. Ask for a few student volunteers to help you show the jobs of plant parts. Let different students take turns showing how they think this works.

★ **English Language Support**—This kinesthetic activity is a perfect way for English language learners to participate in the lesson. They will use their bodies to show what they know. After a few students have modeled this, invite language learners to participate when they feel comfortable.

- First, have three students come to the front of the room to act like the roots of a plant. Students can lie down or curve their bodies around to be the roots. Explain that the roots hold the plant in the soil and bring in water and nutrients.

- Then, have one student volunteer to be the stem. He or she should stand in the place where the stem would be (above the roots). Explain that the stem of the plant carries the water and nutrients to the rest of the plant and holds up the leaves and flower.

- Next, have a few students volunteer to be the leaves of the plant. Students should try to make their bodies look like the leaves of the plant. Explain that the leaves of the plant absorb sunlight and make food.

- Next, have a student volunteer to be the flower of the plant. This student should extend his or her arms and hands above the stem. Explain that the flower makes new seeds.

Parts of a Plant

- Finally, have a few students volunteer to be seeds. They should take their place near the flower. Explain that the seeds drop off or are blown off the flower. The seeds make new plants where they land in the soil.

❸ Tell students that they will choose a plant to research. As a class, brainstorm a list of plants from different habitats that students might be interested in (e.g., cactus, rose, or kelp) and list them on the board. Distribute copies of the *Parts of a Plant Student Notes* activity sheet (page 120) to students and have them complete it while researching information on their plant. Review the sheet as a class and answer any questions that students may have. Schedule time in the library or computer lab for students to research their plant.

❹ Explain to students that they will choose a project to demonstrate their understanding of plant parts and their functions. Distribute copies of the *Parts of a Plant Projects* activity sheet (page 121) to students. Go over each project option with students. You may wish to offer students the option of working independently or with a friend. Allow students time to work on their projects in class.

❺ Distribute copies of the *Parts of a Plant Parent Letter* and the *Parent Assessment* (page 122) for students to take home. Students should prepare for their presentations at home. Have parents complete an assessment of the projects to show what they believe their children learned as a result of practicing for their presentation.

❻ After the projects are due, have students share their projects with the class, identify the plant parts and their functions, and explain how the plant's parts help it survive in its environment.

❼ If students finish early, they may complete the Anchor Activity.

Assessment

Use the *Parts of a Plant Rubric* (page 123) to evaluate students' projects.

Anchor Activity

Have students make an advertisement for a new type of plant that can survive anywhere. Their ad should include a picture of the new plant and a description of how the plant's parts help it survive.

Name _____

Parts of a Plant Student Notes

Directions: Choose a plant to learn more about. Use this sheet to record information about your plant.

Projects are due: _____

1. Type of plant: _____ .

2. Function of the plant's parts:

   - leaf: _____

   - root: _____

   - stem: _____

   - flower: _____

   - seed: _____

3. How my plant survives in its environment:

   _____

   _____

   _____

4. Here is a drawing of my plant in its environment:

© *Shell Education*

Name _____

Parts of a Plant Projects

Directions: Choose a project from the list below to complete. You will present your project to the class.

Projects are due: _____

 Verbal/Linguistic

Write a shape poem to tell about the parts of your plant. Draw an outline of your plant. Inside the drawing, write about each part and what it does. Outside the drawing, write about how it survives in its environment.

 Logical/Mathematical

Make a numbers list of your plant. List each part and how many of that part the plant has. Next to each part, tell what it does and how it helps the plant survive in its environment. Make a numbers list of the plant's environment. For example, list the average temperature or average annual rainfall in its habitat.

 Visual/Spatial

Use art supplies to make a model of your plant. Label each part with its name, what it does, and how the part helps the plant survive in its environment.

 Bodily/Kinesthetic

Make a costume for yourself to dress up as your plant. Prepare a speech for the class from the plant's point of view, explaining each of your parts and how it helps you survive in your environment.

 Musical/Rhythmic

Make up a song or rhyme that explains the parts of your plant, what they do, and how they help the plant survive in its environment. You can make up your own tune or make up words to a tune you know, such as *Mary Had a Little Lamb*.

 Naturalist

Bring in a real example of your plant. Make a poster-size diagram of your plant that labels each part, and tells what it does and how it helps the plant survive.

Parts of a Plant Parent Letter

Date _____

Dear Parent(s),

     Your child is learning about plant parts, their functions, and how a plant's parts help it survive in its environment. Please help your child choose a plant to study and a project to complete from the *Parts of a Plant Projects* list. The project must address the roots, stem, leaves, flower, and seeds of the plant. Your child will be presenting his or her project to the class, pointing out the plant parts, telling each of their functions, and explaining how his or her specific plant uses its parts to survive in its environment. Please help your child prepare for this presentation by helping him or her practice at home. Please evaluate your child's understanding of this topic by completing the *Parent Assessment* below. Return this assessment with your child's project on the due date.

Sincerely,

_____

Project due date: _____

— —

Parent Assessment

Student's Name: _____

Directions: Check *yes* or *no* for each statement.

1. My child demonstrated knowledge of the parts of a plant.   ❏ yes ❏ no

2. My child completed the project.   ❏ yes ❏ no

3. My child practiced his or her performance at home.   ❏ yes ❏ no

4. My child followed directions in completing the project.   ❏ yes ❏ no

5. The information in the project is correct.   ❏ yes ❏ no

Parent Comments:

_____

_____

Student: _____

Parts of a Plant Rubric

Directions: Use the rubric below to evaluate students' projects.

Criteria	1	2	3	4
Student Notes	Student did not complete any of the plant parts and functions.	Student completed 1–2 of the plant parts and functions.	Student completed 3–4 of the plant parts and functions.	Student completed 5 of the plant parts and functions.
Plant Parts	Student identified no plant parts.	Student identified 1–2 plant parts.	Student identified 3–4 plant parts.	Student identified all the plant parts: leaves, root, stem, flower, and seed.
Plant-Part Functions	Student did not explain any plant-part functions.	Student explained some of the plant-part functions.	Student explained most of the plant-part functions.	Student explained all the plant-part functions.
Plant Survival	Student did not explain how the plant parts help the plant survive in its environment.	Student somewhat explained how the plant parts help the plant survive in its environment.	Student generally explained how the plant parts help the plant survive in its environment.	Student clearly explained how the plant parts help the plant survive in its environment.
Presentation	Student demonstrated little or no effort or preparedness.	Student demonstrated some effort and preparedness.	Student demonstrated effort and preparedness.	Student demonstrated strong effort and preparedness.
Total Score: _____ / 20	**Teacher Comments:**			

Forces and Motion

Differentiation Strategy

 Tiered Assignments

Standards

- Students will know that the position and motion of an object can be changed by pushing or pulling.
- TESOL: Students will use English to obtain, process, construct, and provide subject-matter information in spoken and written form.

Materials

- lesson resources (pages 126–129)
- objects to move (e.g., pencils, toy cars, toy spinning tops)
- digital camera
- printer
- yo-yos
- toy spinning tops
- measuring tapes

Procedures

1. Tell students that *motion* is when something moves. Demonstrate different items in motion, for example, dropping a pencil or pushing a toy car. Explain that a *force* is strength or energy that can cause a change in motion. A force can be a push or a pull.

2. Tell students that a *pushing force* moves something away from you. Demonstrate pushing in a chair. If possible, have all students stand up and push their chairs slightly to model the pushing force. Use a digital camera to take a picture of a student doing this. Print it, and label it with an arrow and the word "push." This can be used for reference as students complete their activities.

3. Ask students to brainstorm other things that they push in order to move them (e.g., door, basketball). Create a T-chart on the board with one column entitled "Push." Add students' ideas to this column of the chart.

4. Tell students that a *pulling force* moves something toward you. Demonstrate pulling a chair out. If possible, have all students stand up and pull their chairs slightly to model the pulling force. Use a digital camera to record this action, and print and label the photograph as was done in Step 2 for the pulling motion.

5. Ask students to brainstorm other things that they would pull to move. Label the other column of the T-chart "Pull" and add students' ideas to this column of the chart.

6. Choose some students to use a yo-yo. Have students identify when a pushing force is causing a change in motion and when a pulling force is causing a change in motion. Next, let the yo-yo unravel and hang from the string. Use a digital camera to take pictures of the following actions: have a student push on the yo-yo to cause motion, and have another student pull on the yo-yo to cause motion.

Forces and Motion

7 Tell students that they will be working on forces and motion activities. Distribute copies of the *Forces and Motion* activity sheets (pages 126–128) to students based on their readiness levels.

★ **English Language Support**—Use the images you took with the digital camera to remind English language learners of forces and motion. Give these learners the appropriate activity sheets and meet with them in small groups to clarify the activities.

Activity Levels
▲
Above Grade Level
■
On Grade Level
●
Below Grade Level

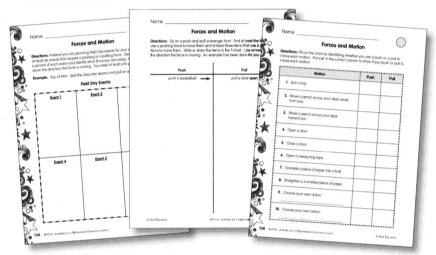

8 If students finish early, they may complete the Anchor Activity.

Assessment

As students work on their activities, walk around the class observing their work. Assess students' understanding of the lesson by filling in the *Forces and Motion Assessment Checklist* (page 129). You will need to ask students to define and identify forces and motion to determine their comprehension of the lesson's content.

Anchor Activity

Have students make a "Forces and Motion in Everyday Life" slide show presentation. First, students will choose a topic of interest, such as sports, music, or transportation. Then, they will provide examples of how forces and motion are used in their topics. Their presentation should include a title and at least five slides illustrating forces and motion. Students must include examples of both pushing and pulling forces and be able to identify which force is being used.

Name _____

Forces and Motion

Directions: Pretend you are planning some Field Day events for your class. Create at least six events that require a pushing or a pulling force. Describe or draw a picture of each event and identify what force you are using. Use arrows to show the direction that the force is moving. You need at least one pulling event.

Example: *Tug-of-War: Split the class into teams and pull on a Tug-of-War rope.*

Field Day Events

Event 1	Event 2	Event 3
Event 4	**Event 5**	**Event 6**

Name _____

Forces and Motion

Directions: Go on a push-and-pull scavenger hunt. Find at least five items that use a pushing force to move them, and at least three items that use a pulling force to move them. Write or draw the items in the T-chart. Use arrows to show the direction that the force is moving. An example has been done for you.

Push	Pull
push a basketball ⟶	*pull a door open* ⟵

Name _____

Forces and Motion

Directions: Fill out the chart by identifying whether you use a push or a pull to cause each motion. Put a checkmark (✔) in the correct column to show if you push or pull to cause each motion.

Motion	Push	Pull
1. Spin a top.		
2. Move a pencil across your desk away from you.		
3. Move a pencil across your desk toward you.		
4. Open a door.		
5. Close a door.		
6. Open a measuring tape.		
7. Crumple a piece of paper into a ball.		
8. Straighten a crumpled piece of paper.		
9. Choose your own action: _____		
10. Choose your own action: _____		

Forces and Motion Assessment Checklist

Teacher Directions: Use the checklist below to assess students' performance. Use check marks (✔) in the criteria columns to indicate proficiency.

Student Name	Defines Force	Defines Motion	Defines Push	Defines Pull	Identifies Push and Pull	Knows Force Causes Change in Motion

Reading Maps

Differentiation Strategy

Tiered Assignments

Standards

• Students will understand the characteristics and uses of maps.

• TESOL: Students will use English to obtain, process, construct, and provide subject-matter information in spoken and written form.

Materials

• lesson resources (pages 132–135)

• "treasure item" (e.g., stickers or pencils)

• chart paper and markers

Procedures

Preparation Note: Hide a "treasure item" somewhere on the playground.

❶ Tell students that you have hidden a treasure on the playground and that you will draw them a map in order for them to find it. On a piece of chart paper or on the board, draw a map of the playground (including the area where you hid the treasure). Tell students that maps typically include a title, a legend with symbols for key landmarks, and a compass rose. Add these items to your map. Explain that landmarks are objects that students will recognize and can be used as guides. School landmarks might include drinking fountains, buildings (such as the auditorium or cafeteria), or specific playground equipment. Note these landmarks on the legend using different symbols.

❷ Label the hidden treasure on the map with an X. Tell students that they will use the map to write directions to the treasure. Have students assist you in writing directions to the X and record their directions on the board.

❸ Define *cardinal directions* (north, south, east, and west) and model how to use them to find the treasure. Rewrite the instructions students gave in Step 2 using cardinal directions. Once the directions are written, have students follow them to find the treasure. The whole class can go together or students can go in small groups if additional adult supervision is available.

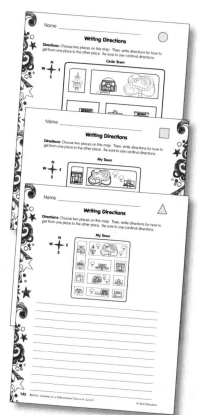

Reading Maps

4 Assign students a shape based on their readiness levels and distribute copies of the appropriate *Writing Directions* activity sheets (pages 132–134) to students. Explain the directions to students and answer any questions that they may have.

★ **English Language Support**—As an added support, partner your English language learners with language-proficient students at the same academic readiness levels for this activity.

5 Once students have completed their activity sheets, have them exchange their maps and directions with partners to see if someone else can accurately follow their directions. Model how to give appropriate feedback to their partners. Address any issues and problems students might have had in writing directions.

6 Tell students that they will make a map of their own, choose a location to hide a treasure, and write directions to get to the treasure. Distribute drawing paper for creating the maps and copies of the *Making a Map* activity sheet (page 135) to students. Students should follow the directions on the activity sheet to create their maps.

7 Have students test their maps and directions with others. Have students trade maps, either within their readiness levels or with students at different readiness levels, and search for each other's treasure.

8 If students finish early, they may complete the Anchor Activity.

Assessment

Evaluate students' maps on their content (title, landmarks indicated, legend with symbols, compass rose) and direction accuracy (the written directions should accurately lead to the "treasure"). You may wish to develop a criteria chart or rubric with students before they begin working so that they understand how their work will be evaluated.

Activity Levels
▲
Above Grade Level
■
On Grade Level
●
Below Grade Level

Anchor Activity

Have students make a map of their country. Students will trace or draw the outline of their country on a sheet of drawing paper. They will locate the state or region in which they live and outline it on the map. Then. they will locate the city in which they live and mark it on the map. Students should include a title, key with symbols, compass rose, and labels. Students will display their completed maps in the classroom.

Name _____

Writing Directions

Directions: Choose two places on this map. Then, write directions for how to get from one place to the other place. Be sure to use cardinal directions.

My Town

_____

_____

_____

_____

_____

_____

_____

_____

_____

_____

_____

Name _____

Writing Directions

Directions: Choose two places on this map. Then, write directions for how to get from one place to the other place. Be sure to use cardinal directions.

My Town

_____

_____

_____

_____

_____

_____

_____

_____

_____

_____

Name _____

Writing Directions

Directions: Choose two places on this map. Then, write directions for how to get from one place to the other place. Be sure to use cardinal directions.

My Town

N
W ✦ E
S

School

Bank

Fire Station

Police

High School

_____

_____

_____

_____

_____

_____

_____

_____

_____

_____

_____

Name _____

Making a Map

Directions: Complete the information below to help you make a map of your classroom.

1. What is the title of your map? _____

2. Think of at least five landmarks to include on your map, for example, your desk. Then, make a symbol for each landmark. Draw the symbols in the correct place on your map. Put symbols in your legend.

   Landmark 1: _____   Symbol 1: _____

   Landmark 2: _____   Symbol 2: _____

   Landmark 3: _____   Symbol 3: _____

   Landmark 4: _____   Symbol 4: _____

   Landmark 5: _____   Symbol 5: _____

3. Draw your map on a sheet of drawing paper. Check off these items as you add them to your map:

   ❐ title

   ❐ landmark symbols on the map

   ❐ legend with symbols

   ❐ compass rose

4. Decide on a small treasure to hide somewhere in the classroom. Choose a place for your treasure on your map. Hide your treasure in the room, and place an *X* on the map in the spot where it is hidden.

5. On the back of your map, give directions to your treasure. Use cardinal directions (north, south, east, and west).

Landforms

Differentiation Strategy

 Leveled Learning Centers

Standards

- Students will know that places can be defined in terms of their predominant human and physical characteristics.
- TESOL: Students will use English to obtain, process, construct, and provide subject-matter information in spoken and written form.

Materials

- lesson resources (pages 138–141)
- pictures of various landforms *(See page 167.)*
- shoe boxes
- art supplies
- glue
- clay
- paint
- foil
- sand
- toothpicks
- construction paper
- scissors

Procedures

Preparation Note: Have students bring in shoe boxes at least one week prior to giving this lesson. Before the lesson, divide the classroom into three centers. Place the following materials at each center:

Center 1—Copies of the *Landforms Advertisement* activity sheet (page 138), art supplies, drawing paper

Center 2—Copies of the *Landforms Models* activity sheet (page 139), shoe boxes, clay, paint, construction paper, foil, sand, toothpicks, drawing paper, glue, scissors

Center 3—Copies of the *Landforms Writing* activity sheet (page 140), lined paper, pencils

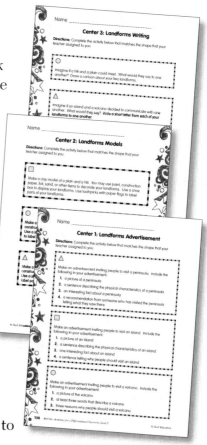

1 Tell students that you are going to play a landform matching game. Collect pictures of different landforms, label each landform, and display them in the classroom.

2 Show students each landform picture and tell them the name of the landform. Tell students to observe the physical characteristics of the landforms and ask them to describe what they see. Have students compare the landforms.

3 Divide the class into four teams. Tell students that you will give them the definition of a landform, and they will have to answer with the type of landform that matches the definition. Each correct answer earns one point. The team with the most points wins. To play, students should raise their hands if they know the answer to a question. Play this game for a few minutes so students become familiar with the landforms.

Landforms

❹ Assign students a shape based on their readiness levels. Explain that students will complete the activity that corresponds to their shape at each center. Review the directions for each center and have students choose where they would like to begin working. Monitor students' progress as they are working and provide assistance, as needed. Once students complete one center, they may move to another.

★ **English Language Support**—Instead of writing answers, have English language learners dictate their answers to you or to language-proficient partners.

❺ As a review activity, distribute copies of the *Landforms Matching Game* activity sheet (page 141) and scissors to students and have them play the matching game with partners.

❻ If students finish early, they may complete the Anchor Activity.

Assessment

Observe students as they work in the centers, and ask questions of them to assess their understanding of the concepts. Keep anecdotal notes on your observations with students' records.

Activity Levels
▲
Above Grade Level
■
On Grade Level
●
Below Grade Level

Anchor Activity

Have students make a landform chart. Students will research landforms that are in their community, their state, and their country. Then, fold a sheet of paper into thirds and label each section *community*, *state*, and *country*. Under each section, students will draw or find pictures of a landform or landforms that can be found in each location.

Name _____

Center 1: Landforms Advertisement

Directions: Complete the activity below that matches the shape that your teacher assigned to you.

Make an advertisement inviting people to visit a peninsula. Include the following in your advertisement:

1. a picture of a peninsula
2. a sentence describing the physical characteristics of a peninsula
3. an interesting fact about a peninsula
4. a recommendation from someone who has visited the peninsula telling what they saw there

Make an advertisement inviting people to visit an island. Include the following in your advertisement:

1. a picture of an island
2. a sentence describing the physical characteristics of an island
3. one interesting fact about an island
4. a sentence telling why people should visit an island

Make an advertisement inviting people to visit a volcano. Include the following in your advertisement:

1. a picture of the volcano
2. at least three words that describe a volcano
3. three reasons why people should visit a volcano

Name _____

Center 2: Landforms Models

Directions: Complete the activity below that matches the shape that your teacher assigned to you.

Make a clay model of a plain and a hill. You may use paint, glue, scissors, construction paper, foil, sand, or other items to decorate your landforms. Use a shoe box to display your landforms. Use toothpicks with paper flags to label parts of your landforms.

Make a clay model of a mountain and a valley. You may use paint, glue, scissors, construction paper, foil, sand, or other items to decorate your landforms. Use a shoe box to display your landforms. Use toothpicks with paper flags to label parts of your landforms.

Make a clay model of a glacier and a plateau. You may use paint, glue, scissors, construction paper, foil, sand, or other items to decorate your landforms. Use a shoe box to display your landforms. Use toothpicks with flags to label parts of your landforms.

Name _____

Center 3: Landforms Writing

Directions: Complete the activity below that matches the shape that your teacher assigned to you.

○

Imagine if a hill and a plain could meet. What would they say to one another? Draw a cartoon about your two landforms.

△

Imagine if an island and a volcano decided to communicate with one another. What would they say? Write a short letter from each of your landforms to one another.

☐

Imagine if a plateau and a peninsula could talk. What would they say to one another? Write a postcard from each of your landforms to one another.

Name _____

Landforms Matching Game

Directions: Cut out the game cards below. Find a partner and spread out the cards face down. The first player chooses two cards. If they match, the player keeps the pair and takes another turn. If the cards do not match, place them back down in the same spots, and have the second player take a turn. When all the cards have been matched, the game is over. The player with the most cards wins.

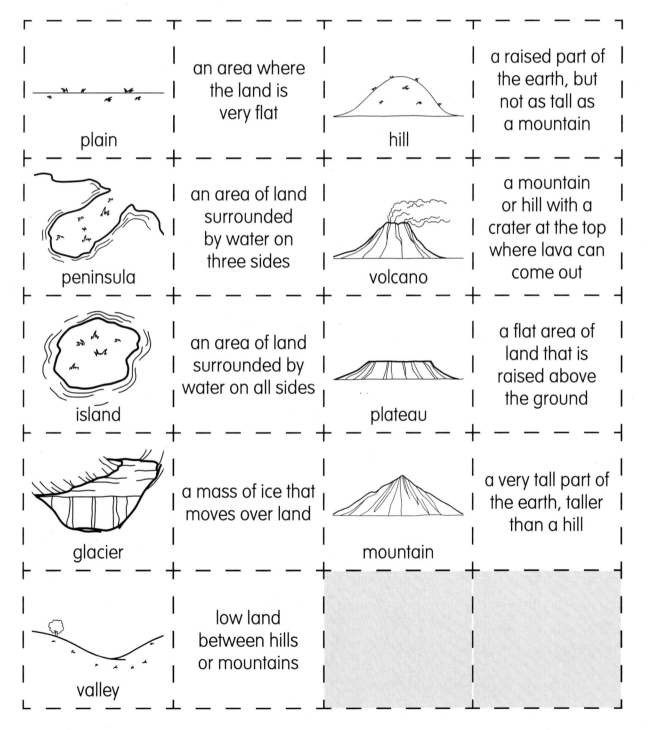

Natural Resources

Differentiation Strategy

 Choices Board

Standards

- Students will know ways in which people depend on the physical environment.

- TESOL: Students will use English to obtain, process, construct, and provide subject-matter information in spoken and written form.

Materials

- lesson resources (pages 144–147)

- chart paper and markers

- one book about natural resources (See page 167.)

- art supplies

- pocket chart (optional)

Procedures

1 Tell students that they will be studying natural resources. Explain that a *natural resource* is something found in nature that people can use. Natural resources include water, air, rocks, soil, trees, and plants. Brainstorm natural resources with students and write their responses on a class chart.

2 Read a book about natural resources to students. Discuss ways that people use natural resources. What are some effects on the environment? Record student responses on a class chart.

3 Have students draw a picture of something they use every day that they could not live without. What natural resource is used in order to have that item? Have students share their pictures and discuss what resources they are using.

4 Assign students a shape based on their readiness levels.

5 Cut apart the *Natural Resources Choices Cards* activity sheets (pages 145–147) and display them on a pocket chart or bulletin board. Tell students that they will be choosing two activities about natural resources from the choices board. Read aloud the activities and answer any questions that students might have.

★ **English Language Support**—Meet with English language learners in a small group to explain directions and assist with writing projects.

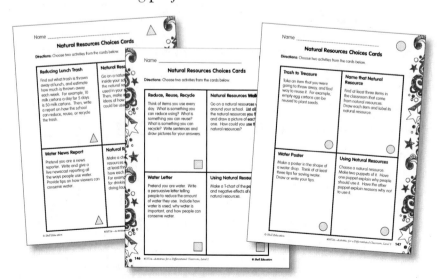

Natural Resources

6 Distribute copies of the *Natural Resources Choices Board* activity sheet (page 144) to students. Have below-grade-level students choose a circle activity to complete individually and a square activity to complete with a friend. Have on-grade-level students choose a square activity to complete individually and a triangle activity to complete with a friend. Have above-grade-level students choose two triangle activities to complete, one individually and one with a friend.

7 When students complete their activities, have them present one project to their classmates.

Activity Levels
▲
Above Grade Level
■
On Grade Level
●
Below Grade Level

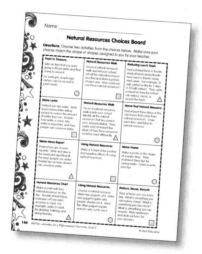

8 If students finish early, they may complete the Anchor Activity.

Assessment

Evaluate the projects that students complete from the choices board to determine whether the lesson objectives were met. Plan to reteach lessons to small groups, as necessary.

Anchor Activity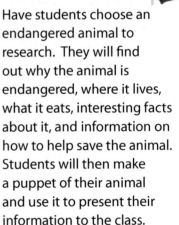

Have students choose an endangered animal to research. They will find out why the animal is endangered, where it lives, what it eats, interesting facts about it, and information on how to help save the animal. Students will then make a puppet of their animal and use it to present their information to the class.

Name _____

Natural Resources Choices Board

Directions: Choose two activities from the choices below. Make sure your choices match the shape or shapes assigned to you by your teacher.

Trash to Treasure Take an item that you were going to throw away and find a way to reuse it. For example, empty egg cartons can be reused to plant seeds. ○	**Natural Resources Walk** Go on a natural resources walk around your school. List all the natural resources you find and draw a picture of each one. How could you use these natural resources? ▢	**Reducing Lunch Trash** Find out what trash is thrown away at lunch and estimate how much is thrown away each week. For example, 10 milk cartons a day for 5 days is 50 milk cartons. Then, write a report on how the school can reduce, reuse, or recycle the trash. △
Water Letter Pretend you are water. Write a persuasive letter telling people to reduce the amount of water they use. Include how water is used, why water is important, and how people can conserve water. ▢	**Natural Resources Walk** Go on a natural resources walk inside your school. Identify all the natural resources that are used in your school building. Then, make a list of at least five ideas of how these resources could be used differently. △	**Name that Natural Resource** Find at least three items in the classroom that come from natural resources. Draw each item, and label its natural resource. ○
Water News Report Pretend that you are a news reporter. Write and give a live newscast reporting all the ways that people use water. Provide tips on how viewers can conserve water. △	**Using Natural Resources** Make a T-chart of the positive and negative effects of using natural resources. ▢	**Water Poster** Make a poster in the shape of a water drop. Think of at least three tips for saving water. Draw or write your tips. ○
Natural Resources Chart Make a chart with four natural resources on the top. Provide at least three examples of how each resource is used. For example, water is used for drinking, bathing, and doing laundry. △	**Using Natural Resources** Choose a natural resource. Make two puppets of it. Have one puppet explain why people should use it. Have the other puppet explain reasons why *not* to use it. ○	**Reduce, Reuse, Recycle** Think of items that you use every day. What is something you can reduce using? What is something you can reuse? What is something you can recycle? Write sentences and draw pictures for your answers. ▢

Name _____

Natural Resources Choices Cards

Directions: Choose two activities from the cards below.

Reducing Lunch Trash

Find out what trash is thrown away at lunch, and estimate how much is thrown away each week. For example, 10 milk cartons a day for 5 days is 50 milk cartons. Then, write a report on how the school can reduce, reuse, or recycle the trash.

Natural Resources Walk

Go on a natural resources walk inside your school. Identify all the natural resources that are used in your school building. Then, make a list of at least five ideas of how these resources could be used differently.

Water News Report

Pretend that you are a news reporter. Write and give a live newscast reporting all the ways that people use water. Provide tips on how viewers can conserve water.

Natural Resources Chart

Make a chart with four natural resources on the top. Provide at least three examples of how each resource is used. For example, water is used for drinking, bathing, and doing laundry.

Name _____

Natural Resources Choices Cards

Directions: Choose two activities from the cards below.

Reduce, Reuse, Recycle

Think of items that you use every day. What is something you can reduce using? What is something you can reuse? What is something you can recycle? Write sentences and draw pictures for your answers.

Natural Resources Walk

Go on a natural resources walk around your school. List all the natural resources you find and draw a picture of each one. How could you use these natural resources?

Water Letter

Pretend you are water. Write a persuasive letter telling people to reduce the amount of water they use. Include how water is used, why water is important, and how people can conserve water.

Using Natural Resources

Make a T-chart of the positive and negative effects of using natural resources.

Name _____

Natural Resources Choices Cards

Directions: Choose two activities from the cards below.

Trash to Treasure

Take an item that you were going to throw away, and find way to reuse it.

For example, empty egg cartons can be reused to plant seeds.

Name that Natural Resource

Find at least three items in the classroom that come from natural resources. Draw each item and label its natural resource.

Water Poster

Make a poster in the shape of a water drop. Think of at least three tips for saving water. Draw or write your tips.

Using Natural Resources

Choose a natural resource. Make two puppets of it. Have one puppet explain why people should use it. Have the other puppet explain reasons why *not* to use it.

Government

Differentiation Strategy

 Menu of Options

Standards

- Students will know that people in positions of authority have limits on their authority.
- TESOL: Students will use English to obtain, process, construct, and provide subject matter information in spoken and written form.

Materials

- lesson resources (pages 150–153)
- scissors
- art supplies
- ballot box
- books and websites about government (See page 167.)

Procedures

Preparation Note: Prepare a Voter Registration Card for each student. Make copies of the *Voter Registration Card* activity sheet (page 150) and cut apart the cards.

1 At the end of a government unit, tell students that they are going to have an election for a class mascot. Each student must design a mascot for the class. Give students time to create their mascots.

2 Tell students that they will explain to the class why their mascot should win the election. Provide time for students to present their mascots to the class.

3 Each student should fill out a Voter Registration Card to prepare to vote. Model for students how to fill out the card, assisting them with the names and spellings of the state and county. Explain that in the United States, everyone age 18 and older has the right to vote. People who want to vote must *register*, or sign up, to vote in their county.

4 Hold a class election. Have students complete a ballot by writing the name of their favorite mascot on a slip of paper and put it into a ballot box. After all the votes have been cast, count the votes and announce the winner of the election.

5 Tell students that they will choose projects to show what they have learned about government. Give each student a *Government Menu of Options* activity sheet (page 151) and review the projects. Answer any questions students may have.

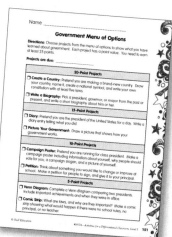

Government

6 Distribute copies of the *Government Menu of Options Planning Chart* activity sheet (page 152) to students. Explain to students that they will need to choose activities that total 25 points. Allow students time to determine which projects they would like to do, and have them fill out the chart.

★ **English Language Support**—Meet separately with English language learners to explain each of the choices and help them fill in their planning charts.

7 Provide students with various art supplies to help them complete their activities. Give students time in class to work on their projects. Schedule visits to the library or computer lab for students to conduct research. When the projects are due, provide time for students to present them to the class. After all students have presented, hold a discussion to summarize what students learned about elections, voting, and the roles of government officials.

8 If students finish early, they may complete the Anchor Activity.

Assessment

Have students complete the *Government Menu of Options Student Self-Assessment* (page 153) to evaluate their work.

Anchor Activity

Have students write a short speech that they would give to Congress about a new law they would like to create. Students will describe their law, explain why it is important, and why they think Congress should vote to pass it.

Voter Registration Cards

Teacher Directions: Copy and cut apart the voter registration cards below and distribute one to each student. Have students fill out their registration cards in order to participate in the class election.

State of _____

Voter Registration Card

County: _____

Name: _____

Age: _____

Address: _____

Signature of Voter: _____

State of _____

Voter Registration Card

County: _____

Name: _____

Age: _____

Address: _____

Signature of Voter: _____

Name _____

Government Menu of Options

Directions: Choose projects from the menu of options to show what you have learned about government. Each project has a point value. You need to earn at least 25 points.

Projects are due: _____

20-Point Projects
☐ **Create a Country:** Pretend that you are making a brand-new country. Draw your country, name it, create a national symbol, and write your own constitution with at least five laws.
☐ **Write a Biography:** Pick a president, governor, or mayor from the past or present, and write a short biography about him or her.

15-Point Projects
☐ **Diary:** Pretend that you are the president of the United States for a day. Write a diary entry telling about what you did.
☐ **Picture Your Government:** Draw a picture that shows how your government works.

10-Point Projects
☐ **Campaign Poster:** Pretend that you are running for class president. Make a campaign poster including information about yourself, why people should vote for you, a campaign slogan, and a picture of yourself.
☐ **Petition:** Think about something you would like to change or improve at school. Make a petition for people to sign, and give it to your principal.

5-Point Projects
☐ **Venn Diagram:** Complete a Venn diagram comparing two presidents. Include important achievements and when they were in office.
☐ **Comic Strip:** What are laws, and why are they important? Make a comic strip showing what would happen if there were no school rules, no principal, or no teacher.

Name _____

Government Menu of Options Planning Chart

Directions: Fill in the chart showing what projects you will complete and what items you will need. Return this to your teacher before beginning your work.

Project Name	Points	Items Needed
Project:		
Project:		
Project:		

Due Date: _____ Total Points: _____

Name _____

Government Menu of Options
Student Self-Assessment

Directions: Circle *yes* or *no* for each statement about your work.

1. I completed a *Government Menu of Options Planning Chart*.	yes	no
2. I followed directions.	yes	no
3. I completed my projects.	yes	no
4. I can identify who is in charge of the national, state, and local governments.	yes	no
5. I know what a law is.	yes	no
6. My projects add up to at least 25 points.	yes	no
7. I did my best.	yes	no

Something interesting I learned is _____ .

I still want to learn_____ .

Historic Figures

Differentiation Strategy

 Tiered Graphic Organizers

Standards

- Students will know regional folk heroes, stories, or songs that have contributed to the development of the cultural history of the U.S.

- TESOL: Students will use English to obtain, process, construct, and provide subject-matter information in spoken and written form.

Materials

- lesson resources (pages 156-159)

- a children's biography about any historic figure (*See page 167.*)

- biographies at different levels (*See page 167.*)

- scissors

- glue or tape

Procedures

Preparation Note: Write the following information on the board:

- *What* explains what was important about that person.

- *Where* explains where he or she was born.

- *When* explains when that person was born, when he or she died, or important events that occurred in his or her life.

- *Why* explains why the person is historic (i.e., historically significant, famous, or important versus merely historical).

- *How* explains the historic person's impact on lives today.

1 Read a children's biography about a historic figure to students. Tell students to think about answering questions like *who, what, where, when, why,* and *how* while listening to the book.

2 As you read, have students discuss the information on the board.

3 Tell students that they will research an important historic figure and record information about that person. Assign students a shape based on their readiness levels.

4 Distribute copies of the *Finding Out About Historic Figures* activity sheets (pages 156–158) to students based on their readiness levels.

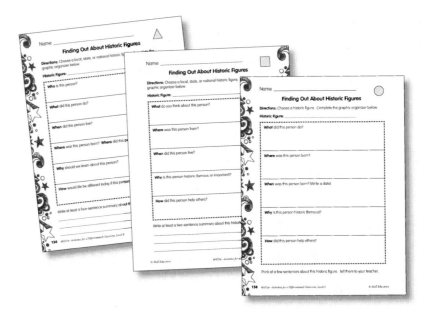

Historic Figures

⑤ Provide leveled biographies for students to use, if possible. Give students time to complete their graphic organizers.

★ **English Language Support**—Have easy-to-read research materials with multiple illustrations available for English language learners. Or, you can select a famous person for these students and read the biography aloud to them, guiding students as they fill in their graphic organizers.

⑥ Have students complete the *Historic Figures Riddle Cube* activity sheet (page 159) by using the information from their graphic organizers. Remind students not to give the name of the person on their cubes; they should only list clues about the person. Instruct students to cut out the cube and assemble it by using tape or glue.

⑦ Have students trade cubes with a partner and try to guess who the famous person is.

⑧ If students finish early, they may complete the Anchor Activity.

Assessment

Review students' graphic organizers and riddle cubes to be sure the lesson objectives were met. Plan mini lessons to reteach the content to small groups of students, as necessary.

Activity Levels
▲
Above Grade Level
■
On Grade Level
●
Below Grade Level

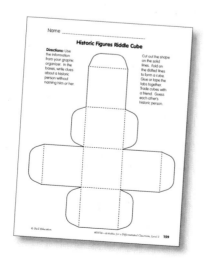

Anchor Activity

Have students choose a second historic figure to learn about. Then, students can create a Venn diagram comparing and contrasting the two people that they researched.

Name _____

Finding Out About Historic Figures

Directions: Choose a local, state, or national historic figure. Complete the graphic organizer below.

Historic Figure: _____

Who is this person?

What did this person do?

When did this person live?

Where was this person born? **Where** did this person live?

Why should we learn about this person?

How would life be different today if this person had not lived?

On a separate sheet of paper, write a four-sentence summary about this historic figure.

Name _____

Finding Out About Historic Figures

Directions: Choose a local, state, or national historic figure. Complete the graphic organizer below.

Historic Figure: _____

What do you think about this person?

Where was this person from?

When did this person live?

Why is this person historic (famous or important)?

How did this person help others?

Write a two-sentence summary about this historic figure.

_____

_____

_____

Name _____

Finding Out About Historic Figures

Directions: Choose a historic figure. Complete the graphic organizer below.

Historic Figure: _____

What did this person do?

Where was this person born?

When was this person born? (Write a date).

Why is this person historic (famous)?

How did this person help others?

Think of a few sentences about this historic figure. Tell them to your teacher.

Historic Figures Riddle Cube

Directions: Use the information from your graphic organizer. In the boxes, write clues about a historic person without naming him or her.

Cut out the shape on the solid lines. Fold on the dotted lines to form a cube. Glue or tape the tabs together. Trade cubes with a friend. Guess each other's historic person.

Economics

Differentiation Strategy

Multiple Intelligences

Standards

- Students will know that people who use goods and services are called consumers, and people who make goods or provide services are called producers, and that most people both produce and consume.

- TESOL: Students will use English to obtain, process, construct, and provide subject-matter information in spoken and written form.

Materials

- lesson resources (pages 162–165)

- scissors

- poster paper

- art supplies

Procedures

1 To culminate a unit of study on economics, students will participate in a Market Day where they will offer a good or a service for sale to other students at school. They will also become consumers and shop at their classmates' stores.

2 Review vocabulary and concepts from the unit with students, as necessary. Students should understand the concepts of producers and consumers, goods and services, and profits and losses.

3 Explain to students that they will produce a good or a service to sell at a class Market Day. Other classes will be invited to attend Market Day as customers. You may wish to build enthusiasm for the event by deciding as a class how to spend the Market Day profits. Students may want to earn money for a party, field trip, or charitable cause.

4 Have students brainstorm ideas for goods and services to sell at Market Day. Distribute copies of the *Economics Parent Letter* (page 165) to students and have them take it home. Have students work with their parents to decide on a good or service to sell. You may wish to invite parents to volunteer at Market Day at this time, too. Students should prepare their goods or services at home and bring them to class on Market Day.

5 Distribute copies of the *Market Day Jobs* activity sheet (page 162) to students and review the different jobs that students need to perform before the actual Market Day event. Provide art supplies and give students time to complete these activities in class.

6 Have students price their items in quarter increments (e.g., $0.75, $1.25, etc.) to make it easier for them to make change on Market Day. To keep the prices low enough, you may want to provide a price limit of what students can charge for a good or service.

7 Distribute copies of the *Economics Receipt for Goods or Services* activity sheet (page 164) to students. Have students fill out the receipts and cut them apart. On Market Day, students should provide a receipt for each of their customers.

8 On Market Day, give students time to set up their stores. Have students push desks together to act as their storefronts, and attach advertising posters as signs. Remind students to be responsible for their products and money.

★ **English Language Support**—Seat English language learners next to language-proficient students to help them communicate with customers. Be prepared to provide extra assistance to these students during Market Day.

9 At the end of the event, allow time for students to clean up their stores. Distribute copies of the *Economics Expense Sheet* activity sheet (page 163) to students. Have students complete the activity sheet to calculate their Market Day profits.

10 If students finish early, they may complete the Anchor Activity.

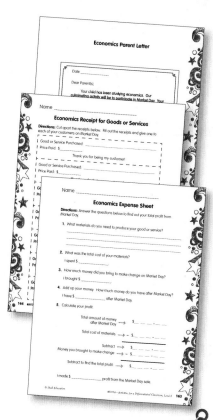

Assessment

Observe students as they plan and carry out Market Day to assess their understanding of economics.

Anchor Activity

Have students make up a commercial for their product or service. They may write a script for the commercial and perform or videotape it to show the class. Students should consider how to attract consumers to their stores and increase their profits with advertising.

Name _____

Market Day Jobs

Directions: Get ready for Market Day by completing the activities below.

Market Day date: _____

My good or service will be _____

I will charge _____ **for this good or service.**

📖 Verbal/Linguistic

Marketing: Before Market Day, write an invitation to other classes at school, inviting students to attend Market Day. Explain the product or service you will be selling.

👁 Visual/Spatial

Advertising: Before Market Day, create posters advertising your product or service. Post these around school, and also use one as a sign for your store. Be sure to list the prices of the items you are selling.

🎵 Musical/Rhythmic

Promotion: Make up a jingle to advertise your product or service. Think of popular jingles you have heard on television or radio commercials to get ideas. Visit classrooms before Market Day to perform your jingle and perform it during Market Day, too.

Name _____

Economics Expense Sheet

Directions: Answer the questions below to find out your total profit from Market Day.

1. What materials do you need to produce your good or service?

_____

_____

_____

2. What was the total cost of your materials?

I spent $ _____.

3. How much money did you bring to make change on Market Day?

I brought $ _____.

4. Add up your money. How much money do you have after Market Day?

I have $ _____ after Market Day.

5. Calculate your profit.

Total amount of money ⟶ $__ __ __ . __ __
after Market Day

Total cost of materials ⟶ − $__ __ __ . __ __
_____

Subtract ⟶ $__ __ __ . __ __
Money you brought to make change ⟶ − $__ __ __ . __ __
_____

Subtract to find the total profit: ⟶ $__ __ __ . __ __

I made $ _____ profit from the Market Day sale.

Name _____

Economics Receipt for Goods or Services

Directions: Cut apart the receipts below. Fill out the receipts and give one to each of your customers on Market Day.

Good or Service Purchased: _____

Price Paid: $_____

Thank you for being my customer!

Good or Service Purchased: _____

Price Paid: $_____

Thank you for being my customer!

Good or Service Purchased: _____

Price Paid: $_____

Thank you for being my customer!

Good or Service Purchased: _____

Price Paid: $_____

Thank you for being my customer!

Good or Service Purchased: _____

Price Paid: $_____

Thank you for being my customer!

Good or Service Purchased: _____

Price Paid: $_____

Thank you for being my customer!

Good or Service Purchased: _____

Price Paid: $_____

Thank you for being my customer!

Economics Parent Letter

Date _____

Dear Parent(s),

     Your child has been studying economics. Our culminating activity will be to participate in Market Day. Your child will produce and provide a good or a service to sell to other students at school. Your child will need to spend some time at home preparing his or her goods or the materials for his or her service.

     Each student will advertise his or her good or service by creating invitations addressed to classes in the school, producing poster advertisements, and writing a jingle for their good or service. These activities will be completed at school. On Market Day, your child will set up his or her booth and handle the money. Your child will need to bring about $2.00 in quarters to Market Day in order to make change. Your child may also bring additional money for purchasing items from other students' stores.

     Your child will be responsible for making change for his or her customers, so please practice this skill at home. Thank you in advance for your support.

Please have goods or services ready for Market Day on

_____.

Sincerely,

_____

References

Bess, J. 1997. *Teaching well and liking it: Motivating faculty to teach effectively.* Baltimore, MD: Johns Hopkins University Press.

Brandt, R. 1998. *Powerful learning.* Alexandria, VA: Association for Supervision and Curriculum Development.

Bruner, J. 2004. *Toward a theory of instruction.* Cambridge, MA: Belnap Press of Harvard University Press.

Costa, A. L., and R. Marzano. 1987. Teaching the language of thinking. *Educational Leadership* 45: 29–33.

Gardner, H. 1983. *Frames of mind: The theory of multiple intelligences.* New York: Basic Books.

———. 1999. *Intelligence reframed: Multiple intelligences for the 21st Century.* New York: Basic Books.

Jensen, E. 1998. *Teaching with the brain in mind.* Alexandria, VA: Association for Supervision and Curriculum Development.

Kaplan, S. N. 2001. Layering differentiated curriculum for the gifted and talented. In *Methods and materials for teaching the gifted*, ed. F. Karnes and S. Bean, 133–158. Waco, TX: Prufrock Press.

Olsen, K. D. 1995. *Science continuum of concepts: For grades K–6.* Black Diamond, WA: Books for Educators.

Sprenger, M. 1999. *Learning and memory: The brain in action.* Alexandria, VA: Association for Supervision and Curriculum Development.

Teele, S. 1994. Redesigning the educational system to enable all students to succeed. PhD diss., University of California, Riverside.

Winebrenner, S. 1992. *Teaching gifted kids in the regular classroom.* Minneapolis, MN: Free Spirit Publishing.

Additional Resources

Where books and websites are referenced in lesson materials lists, some suggestions for these resources are provided below. Shell Education does not control the content of these websites, or guarantee their ongoing availability, or links contained therein. We encourage teachers to preview these websites before directing students to use them.

Page 28—Vocabulary

McIlwain, John. *DK Children's Illustrated Dictionary*. New York: DK Children, 2009.

Root, Betty. *My First Picture Dictionary: 1,000 Words, Pictures, and Definitions*. New York: DK Children, 1993.

Page 34—Reader's Response

Na, Il Sung. *A Book of Sleep*. New York: Knopf Books for Young Readers, 2009.

Pinkney, Larry. *The Lion and the Mouse*. Boston: Little, Brown Books for Young Readers, 2009.

www.bpl.org/kids/booksmags.htm

http://frost.monroe.lib.in.us/childrens/booklists

Page 40—Persuasive Texts

Keats, Ezra Jack. *Pet Show!* New York: Puffin, 2001.

Orloff, Karen Kaufman. *I Wanna Iguana*. New York: G.P. Putnam's Sons, 2004.

Provensen, Alice. *Our Animal Friends at Maple Hill Farm*. New York: Aladdin, 2001.

Page 46—Poetry

Prelutsky, Jack. *The Random House Book of Poetry for Children*. New York: Random House, 1983.

Young, Judy. *R is for Rhyme: A Poetry Alphabet*. Ann Arbor, MI: Sleeping Bear Press, 2010.

www.fizzyfunnyfuzzy.com

Page 52—Research

Adler, David A. *A Picture Book of Amelia Earhart*. New York: Holiday House, 1999.

————. *A Picture Book of Harriet Tubman*. New York: Holiday House, 2003.

Rau, Dana Meachen. *Dr. Seuss*. Danbury, CT: Children's Press, 2003.

www.biography.com

Page 136—Landforms

http://geology.about.com/library/bl/images/bllandformindex.htm

Page 142—Natural Resources

Barraclough, Sue. *Earth's Resources*. Portsmouth, NH: Heinemann Library, 2008.

Bauman, Amy. *Earth's Natural Resources*. New York: Gareth Stevens Publishing, 2008.

Page 148—Government

Sobel, Syl. *How the U.S. Government Works*. Hauppauge, New York: Barron's Educational Series, 1999.

www.kids.gov

Page 154—Historic Figures

Adler, David A. Picture Book Biography series. New York: Holiday House.

Rookie Biographies series. Danbury, CT: Children's Press.

www.biography.com

www.history.com

Contents of the Teacher Resource CD

Lesson Resource Pages

Page	Lesson	Filename
24–27	Punctuation Rules!	pg024.pdf
30–33	Vocabulary	pg030.pdf
36–39	Reader's Response	pg036.pdf
42–45	Persuasive Texts	pg042.pdf
48–51	Poetry	pg048.pdf
54–57	Research	pg054.pdf
60–63	Patterns in Nature	pg060.pdf
66–69	Number Sense	pg066.pdf
72–75	Money	pg072.pdf
78–81	Measurement	pg078.pdf
84–87	Shapes	pg084.pdf
90–93	Fractions	pg090.pdf
96–99	Earth, Moon, and Sun	pg096.pdf
102–105	Water Cycle	pg102.pdf
108–111	Properties of Matter	pg108.pdf
114–117	Animals	pg114.pdf
120–123	Parts of a Plant	pg120.pdf
126–129	Forces and Motion	pg126.pdf
132–135	Reading Maps	pg132.pdf
138–141	Landforms	pg138.pdf
144–147	Natural Resources	pg144.pdf
150–153	Government	pg150.pdf
156–159	Historic Figures	pg156.pdf
162–165	Economics	pg162.pdf

Teacher Resources

Title	Filename
Answer Key	answers.pdf
Comic Strip	comic.pdf
Flow Chart	flow.pdf
Hundred Chart	hundred.pdf
T-Chart	tchart.pdf
Three Column Chart	threecolumn.pdf
Time Line	timeline.pdf
Triple Venn Diagram	Triplevenn.pdf
Venn Diagram	venn.pdf